Advance praise for

GREG BOGART's wonderful new book gracefully opens the door to an understanding of higher frequency astrology. Viewing the horoscope as a journey of growth potential—instead of fatalistic determinism—moves the reader toward inner wisdom and empowerment. As a therapeutic astrologer, I particularly appreciate Greg's perspective—that the planetary cycles (transits and solar arcs) affecting the natal chart offer opportunities for powerful personal development. The rhythmic movement of the planets helps us to achieve our life purpose—to refine and polish the soul. And his chapter connecting astrology to music is brilliant! I've often experienced astrology as musical chord progression and tonal discord yearning for resolution. Greg invites us to integrate all of our senses and resonate with the horoscope, and we're indeed led to a higher octave of experience and understanding. I have high praise and deep respect for this book, so mindfully written and beautifully communicated, and I recommend it to anyone interested in the fine art and genuine craft of astrology. **—Kathy Rose, Roseastrology.com**

COMBINING SPIRITUAL PSYCHOLOGY, astrology, yoga philosophies, and conscious dreamwork, this book is conversational and personal—not another astrological cookbook. I picked up unique gems of interpretation in this enjoyable read, geared toward professional astrologers yet suitable for all serious students of the craft. The final section on astrology and music is particularly fresh and inspirational. **—Kay Taylor, Author of *Soul Path Way***

GREG'S PIONEERING work in the integration of astrology and psychotherapy is a huge support and inspiration to those of us on this path. Here Greg speaks with the voice of a Wise Elder. **—Andrea Conlon, M.S.W., Astrologer and Psychotherapist**

GREG BOGART's masterful understanding of archetypes, dreamwork, and the power of sound offer a unique window into how astrology can help awaken and transform consciousness. Through sharing personal experiences as well as many examples from his client work, he eloquently illustrates how astrology is an invaluable tool in emotional healing, vocational guidance, and a method of enriching all areas of daily life. The breadth, depth, and originality of Greg's insights in *Astrology's Higher Octaves* will be valuable to both seasoned professionals as well as beginners interested in a very grounded, yet deeply spiritual approach to astrology. —**Stephanie Austin, M.A., Ecoastrology.com**

GREG BOGART has provided the counseling astrologer a roadmap for sharing the practical and spiritual message of the planets to help clients make decisions in tune with their core values. He shows how astrological patterns shape each person's path forward, transforming everyday events into an evolution of consciousness. —**Carol Tebbs, former President of Kepler College**

GREG BOGART has written a book that's bound to become a classic in our field. Some astrology books are instructive, some fun to read; *Astrology's Higher Octaves* is both. Without reservation, I recommend it to all of my colleagues. It will be on my reading list for my correspondence school. Greg's way of explaining the techniques he uses is simple; the case studies concisely illustrate his points. He weaves together therapy, astrology, and musical cosmology in a refreshing way. It's one of those very few astrology books worth more than a single reading. —**Bob Mulligan, Author of** *Between Astrologers and Clients*

WRITTEN BY one of the most experienced astrologers, authors, and psychotherapists today, *The Astrology's High Octaves* is a masterful and much needed compendium of the therapeutic uses of astrology. For the psychotherapist and astrological counselor alike, it describes how astrological archetypes can open up paths for healing. Dr. Bogart illustrates how clients can participate with their charts by yielding to the meanings that arise synchronistically in planetary symbols and in life. Clients can then attune to the presiding energies and make choices for their own betterment. The psyche of the client and the astrological symbols collaborate in the healing process and attain a kind of Dao of astrology. —**Gisele Terry, Marriage and Family Therapist, former President of International Society for Astrological Research**

THIS BOOK provides a multi-layered approach to astrology as a tool to understand and evolve the human psyche. It addresses the astrology of emotional healing and therapy, relationships, dream analysis, vocational orientation, and then sound and harmonies, weaving these components into a holistic vision. Author Greg Bogart details each of these layers using examples of public figures, clients, and his own life anecdotes, emphasizing practical application of this higher knowledge. Greg's eloquence makes this a truly captivating and insightful read. — **Maurice Fernandez, President, The Organization for Professional Astrology**

WITH GRACE AND WISDOM, Greg Bogart passes on his knowledge of how to use astrology with clients and for self-growth. This is a manual for the next generation of astrologers, but even the most experienced practitioners will find new ideas as the text builds to a crescendo with the chapter on music and astrology. —**Arlan Wise, Vice President, The Organization for Professional Astrology**

WITH THE reemergence of technique-driven, formulaic systems in our field, it is more important than ever that we consultant astrologers have a person-centred, therapeutic approach to horoscope interpretation. In order to help others, we must know how to articulate the birth chart and be in dialogue with clients. In this masterful, illuminating book, Greg Bogart guides the reader with compassion, authority and wisdom towards these important goals. In particular, his work synthesising astrology with career counseling theory demonstrates how we can use astrology to navigate career cycles and professional crises, and to express our talents while accomplishing our inner calling in the outer world. —**Frank Clifford, Principal of the London School of Astrology**

BOOKS BY GREG BOGART

Planets in Therapy: Predictive Technique and the Art of Counseling

Astrology and Spiritual Awakening

*Therapeutic Astrology: Using the Birth Chart in Psychotherapy
and Spiritual Counseling*

Astrology and Meditation: The Fearless Contemplation of Change

In the Company of Sages: The Journey of the Spiritual Seeker

Dreamwork and Self-Healing

Dreamwork in Holistic Psychotherapy of Depression

Finding Your Life's Calling

The Nine Stages of Spiritual Apprenticeship

Astrology's Higher Octaves

New Dimensions of a Healing Art

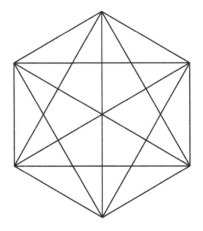

Greg Bogart, Ph.D.

Ibis Press
Lake Worth, FL

Published in 2020 by Ibis Press
A division of Nicolas-Hays, Inc.
P. O. Box 540206
Lake Worth, FL 33454-0206
www.ibispress.net

Distributed to the trade by
Red Wheel/Weiser, LLC
65 Parker St. • Ste. 7
Newburyport, MA 01950
www.redwheelweiser.com

ISBN: 978-0-89254-193-5
Ebook: 978-0-89254-679-4

Library of Congress Cataloging-in-Publication Data
Available upon request

Book design and production by Studio 31
www.studio31.com

[BP]

Printed in the United States of America

Contents

Acknowledgements

The writings in this volume originated in presentations to San Francisco Astrological Society, NCGR San Francisco & New York, United Astrology Conference, International Society for Astrological Research, The Organization for Professional Astrology, Rocky Mountain Astrologers, and International Astrology Day SF. I'm grateful for the opportunity to develop this work in collaboration with these organizations.

I'd like to thank a number of friends and colleagues who have been key allies during the writing and production of this book: Rick Amaro, Stephanie Austin, Lynn Bell, Naomi Bennett, Agneta Borstein, Ken Bowser and Colleen Mauro, Nancy Carleton, Frank Clifford, Cathy Coleman, Andrea Conlon, Armand Diaz, Maurice Fernandez, Steven Forrest, Robert Forte, Ray Grasse, Dennis Harness, Tony Howard, Brad Kochunas, Michael Lutin, Tad Mann, Ray Merriman and Antonia Langsdorf, Charles Mintz and Julie Garfield, Shelley Montie, Bob Mulligan, Gayle Peterson, Steve Pincus, Kathy Rose, Sandra-Leigh Serio, Ed Snow, Tem Tarriktar and Kate Sholly, Kay Taylor, Carol Tebbs, Gisele Terry, Linea Van Horn, and Arlan Wise.

I also thank my wife, Diana Syverud, for her wisdom and steady encouragement. And I feel fortunate indeed to have my writing presented by Ibis Press and warmly thank Deborah DeNicola, James Wasserman, and Yvonne Paglia.

Preface

As esoteric as it seems to some people, astrology is actually very down-to-earth—a discipline blending mysticism and pragmatism for the enhancement of life. Intelligent astrologers use this knowledge to get their lives organized, to flow through life gracefully and skillfully, meeting goals and coping with adversities, growing in consciousness through each challenge. The imaginal, the strategic, and the magical converge as we, the conscious astrologer, become established in the *bindu*, the point of consciousness, seat of visualization and manifestation.

As much as I resisted the very idea of the subject at first, the doctrines, worldview, and practices of astrology have been a positive, beautiful influence in my life. This knowledge has been the guiding pole star steering me through many changes and events, shaping my vision and affecting me on many levels, in different domains. Now, after almost 40 years as a practitioner, I'm taking this opportunity to describe several different ways I apply astrology in my life and in my work as a counselor. In this book I describe how astrology enhances the enjoyment of daily activities, facilitates emotional healing and transformative life review, synchronizes with the archetypal symbolism and vivid messages of dreams, guides the development of careers, and teaches us to discover and express the distinctive vibrational tones and music of the individual personality. I also touch on the connection of astrology with the broader tradition of esotericism and its emphasis on transformation through the practice of creative imagination.

I have always found that astrology fosters skillfulness and accomplishment. Awareness of each day's transiting planets helps guide my attention to the full spectrum of everyday tasks with a sharpened sense of purpose and meaning. This idea is the basis for the technique of Diurnal Astrology, a method that bolsters our practical intelligence and efficiency in daily life, the topic of Chapter 4.

Astrology is a beacon to me in the relational sphere, shedding light on patterns of relating, the phases and seasons of relationships, the cyclical changing moods, and the planetary laws of attraction that are linked to the cycles of Venus and Mars. Knowledge of my astrological profile and traits, and of current transits, along with consideration of the natal traits and current challenges of a spouse, friend, parent, or child—all of this creates a basis for more emotionally fulfilling and more committed relationships with others. I spelled this out in *Planets in Therapy*, Part IV, on the topic of Synastry and Conscious Relationships, and throughout this present volume we'll study examples of how astrological work can aid an individual's or a couple's understanding of relational experiences and patterns of behavior. We learn how relationships have been damaged; we envision ways they might be repaired.

Knowledge of astrology is also immensely helpful in the realm of work and career development, informing us about optimal career paths and the meaning our work has for us at different life stages; it provides wise perspective on the pressures and stresses most people experience regarding work and employment. Chapter 5 describes my approach to the practice of vocational astrology to skillfully guide oneself and others in the world of work. This is one of the key areas of our societal life where the services of astrologers can be most impactful and will probably be in greatest future demand. I show how vocational astrology is enhanced through knowledge of several career counseling theories, discuss how astrology aids us through periods of career crisis, and correlate planetary symbols with the renowned John Holland Typology of six vocational types.

My own occupational path has involved creating a hybrid identity as a professional astrologer and a licensed Marriage and Family Therapist—a therapeutic astrologer and an astrologically informed psychotherapist. In two earlier books, *Therapeutic Astrology* and *Planets in Therapy*, I described how to integrate analysis of the birth chart and transits to give focus to the counseling process and to gain refined understanding of personality characteristics, key life themes, and highly charged complexes. This present work seeks to further this synthesis with additional examples and some new directions. Encapsulating some key features and assumptions of therapeutic astrology, emphasizing a developmental and process-oriented approach, I describe several characteristics of transformative chart interpretation and invite readers to apply these principles in their own astrological studies and practice.

Many people have a preconceived image of astrology as a system of static personality descriptions and typing of persons based on sun signs. But to me, astrology never feels static. Unexpected things happen in sessions of astrological process work where we contemplate the birth chart and transits to explore feelings and memories, imagine desired behavioral and attitudinal changes, and script out the anticipated timing. The revelation of meanings is spontaneous and often startling.

One avenue I've discovered for dynamic process work involves the union of astrology and dream analysis. As a psychotherapist I'm very interested in dreams and their healing messages, and I've authored two books on Jungian dreamwork as a treatment modality.[1] What I find especially efficacious is to identify links between dream symbols and planetary symbols and thereby step into the accelerating evolutionary force field of various archetypes—patterns of change and transformation. Combining astrology and dream interpretation tunes us into what is happening within the unconscious mind, which is a place where change originates. Chapter 3 explores how dream images and narratives reflect astrological symbolism, and how this can irradiate dreams with spiritual meanings. Interpreting the symbolism of astrology and dreams together and relating these to our current situation brings the transformative archetypes into life, into the body. Several examples will demonstrate that astrological dreamwork holds great promise as a component of the spiritual psychotherapy of the future.

Later, I assert that not only does astrology aid us in managing the practical business of life, work, and relationships, it's also a practice that refines us vibrationally in a manner analogous to music. The final chapter on Sound of the Cosmos: Astrology and Music in the Evolution of Consciousness stems from my lifelong growth as a musician—an interest that reflects my natal Venus conjunct Sun and Moon, Venus square Neptune, and Venus trine Ascendant. I show how astrology is enhanced through drawing analogies to music, and that our evolution has discernible pulse, melodies, harmonies, and dissonance. This chapter is a meditation on the union of two of our most uplifting and rejuvenating human activities.

The tantric thread that runs through these variegated aspects of astrological practice is that in all of these realms of work, daily life, and in dream narratives, we experience *the living archetype manifest in time*. Archetypes are the key structures of human consciousness—for example, the hero's journey; they are luminous fibers woven into the fabric of time. Astrology shows that the manifestation of archetypes has predictable organization and identifiable timing. We experience how archetypes, recurrent patterns of experience and behavior, identified by Jung, are present in the here and now, pointing the way, showing us the shape transformation wants to take. Astrologers observe and experience the living archetypes constantly emerging in daily occurrences, in synchronicities and dreams. I believe the astrological study of archetypes manifesting in time is a master key to worldly success and spiritual enlightenment. [2]

This book describes several facets of my approach to practicing this sacred art—an approach that suits my personality and interests, my Uranian quirks and idiosyncracies. I've completed this work while transiting Uranus is opposite my natal Jupiter in the 1st house, so I find myself writing at times in the first person, describing what I personally believe, what is true for me. I present my vision of astrology—a therapeutic healing art, a means of enhanced human relationships; a tool for focused, effective career counseling; a daily teacher of impeccability in the course and conduct of life; a path of self-transformation and a spiritual training that refines our internal organization, so the personality expresses distinctive tones. I seek to unify the practical, vocational, depth psychological, and vibrational aspects of astrology's prismatic wisdom, sounding tones encompassing multiple octaves.

CHAPTER 1
Points of Departure:
Becoming a Therapeutic Astrologer

I began to develop an astrologer's worldview in my early twenties while transiting Uranus squared natal Sun and Moon and also squared its natal position in my 10th house; and while Neptune was conjunct natal Saturn in Sagittarius. Those Neptune and Uranus transits indicated a period of personal liberation and discovery of the sacred, individuation and internal self-offering to the spirit. I experienced several years of occupational vagueness and uncertainty while devoting myself to spirituality, yoga practices, metaphysical studies, and filling notebooks with drawings, poems, and elaborate dream interpretations. In 1980, after being introduced to my birth map and transits by several teachers and some introductory books, I took an ephemeris out into the woods and slept outdoors over the course of months, which allowed me to track phases of the Moon, her visible conjunctions with planets, and I soaked in the beauty of Venus's glorious morning and evening star phases. I gazed at Mars and got in touch with the red, fiery part of myself. I watched Jupiter and Saturn form their momentous conjunction in Libra. I felt the sky and that I was somehow a part of it. I experienced the dissolution and disorientation so characteristic of Neptune transits, but through the fog of uncertainty I sought a spiritual life-path and asked inwardly that I might be rightly guided. That's when I arrived in Boulder, Colorado and serendipitously met Andres Takra, the Sage of Caracas, my astrology teacher and mentor, who was incredibly generous with his knowledge.

I studied with Andres five days a week for nine months, taking instruction and ghost writing his book, *The Wisdom of Sidereal Astrology*. This was in 1981 during the Jupiter-Saturn conjunction in Libra in my 12th house, squaring natal Mercury in Capricorn. This transit changed my life forever. To this day, a principle method I use for chart readings is to track the momentous Jupiter-Saturn conjunctions, which

Andres Boulton Figueira de Mello, AKA Andres Takra,
Astrologer, Author, and Artist

establish life trends and projects that unfold over 20-year periods of development.[3] Alexander Ruperti, author of *Cycles of Becoming*, taught that the Jupiter-Saturn cycle concerns the formation of our social destiny. After this conjunction, for the next 20 years I followed the path of being an astrologer, aspiring musician and songwriter, and yoga student and practitioner. The 12th house can be a gestating womb and a sanctuary, a space of sacred liminality, and during this 12th house Jupiter-Saturn conjunction my inner life was activated through immersion in meditation and depth psychology.[4] For two years I studied Ivy Goldstein-Jacobsen's book on *Simplified Horary Astrology* [5] and I was constantly casting horary charts trying to discern the answers I needed and to understand the mysteries of karma and the symbolic tapestry of time. I found my place in the cosmic matrix, felt myself part of timeless existence and the energies of the spirit world, and discovered my own *axis mundi*.

It wasn't until 20 years later, at age 42, at the next Jupiter-Saturn conjunction in 2000, in Taurus, which fell in my 8th house, that I became materially more grounded, landing a stable teaching job, purchasing a house, and paying a mortgage. Truly, the Jupiter-Saturn conjunctions mark defining moments and formative choices, which can take us onto a completely different life path. Whenever I do chart readings I track the house placement and aspects of the Jupiter-Saturn conjunctions (and oppositions), noting what has manifested in the person's life at those times. Our lives unfold over stretches of decades in resonance with the pulse of this cycle.[6]

Every practitioner is faced with the task of how to organize a life astrologically. At my initial Saturn return, I attended graduate school in counseling psychology, and eventually became a licensed Marriage and Family Therapist, at the time of a Jupiter-Saturn opposition. Transiting Saturn was conjunct my Sun, so this licensure marked an accommodation to societal norms and laid the foundation for my livelihood. Training in counseling skills made me a better astrologer, more knowledgeable about human development, and better equipped to guide people through difficult transits and emotional thickets.

From the beginning I utilized astrology in my clinical practice, joining astrology's mythic symbolism and timing techniques with the process-oriented methods of psychotherapy. I refer to the birth chart and transits to give focus to the counseling process and to help people in states of emotional, psychological, and relational distress.[7] I utilize astrology as part of holistic treatment for depression, anxiety, anger management, substance abuse, and relationship conflicts and impasses.[8] As a therapeutic astrologer, I apply celestial symbolism for emotional healing, for self-integration, and to explore key moments of a person's development and the origins of problems in adjustment. I examine how the archetype of personality shown by the natal chart takes form as a vocation or occupation and use this perspective to provide informed career guidance. Gazing through the horoscope's sharply focused lens I listen to the person's story and reinterpret it. At times the work touches places of emotional pain and fixation, like pressing on a sensitive pressure point; palpating the painful area relieves it, soothing emotional injuries.

I provide a vision of what's possible for each individual, and identify specific strategies for making changes happen. I try to express my interpretations in a way that won't make a person overly anxious about their situation, their present and their future. I don't want my clients to feel that everything is determined by the planets and that they have no control over their destiny. The planets provide a roadmap and a schedule, and we can go places should we choose to board the train.

Having described how I came to practice and formulate this way of applying astrological symbols and techniques, I'll briefly state some core principles of therapeutic astrology and illustrate these with several examples. Astrology's evocative symbolism can be a tremendous catalyst to implement desired behavioral changes and to uplift our lives.

CHAPTER 2

The Purpose and Methods of
Therapeutic Astrology

Technically speaking, when I speak of therapeutic astrology I'm referring to an approach that would be most suitable for astrologers who are also trained counselors and mental health professionals who know about diagnosis, assessment, and treatment methods. But I think anyone who resonates with this approach can utilize astrology therapeutically for psychological maturation and enhanced self-awareness—not just professional psychotherapists. The basic orientation of therapeutic astrology is to study the birth chart and transits to understand key themes and central events of a person's life, to identify significant traumas and sources of stress, to assess current developmental tasks, and to acknowledge passages we're experiencing and their specific meanings. Suffering, struggling, or depressed individuals can learn to understand their situations in the light of planetary symbolism. Maybe they've been subject to the weakening, disorganizing effects of Neptune, which can be exacerbated through alcohol abuse and chemical dependency. Or perhaps a person is struggling to meet the challenges of material life and practical decision-making that are associated with transits of Saturn, whose tests are best satisfied by hard work and sustained effort. Or maybe one is suffering after an unsettling relationship or a breakup during an outer planet transit involving natal Venus. Someone with a difficult stellium of planets in the 4th house may be facing adversities in the family that contribute to their depression and distress. As astrologers, we perceive each person as unfolding within an organized cosmos and glimpse how things appear to happen for a reason, so our suffering and challenges aren't meaningless; they are purposeful and intentional.[9] This powerful navigational tool is available and equally helpful for therapeutic self-study and self-guidance and for use by helping professionals.

I believe that we can uplift mental health care and our personal self-care by integrating meditation, yoga, dreams, and other forms of spirituality—the perception and experience of being part of a larger wholeness. Astrology is founded on that awareness and puts it into practice in every nuance of its doctrines and techniques. It offers a basis for strategic action through time, using a template that's specific to us as individuals. Seeing various areas of life accentuated by planetary transits at specific moments provides a foundation for optimal personal development.

It comes as a surprise to some people that astrology could be relevant to mental health care, as we astrologers are the ones often viewed as slightly nutty. Astrology's critics argue that astrology implies a doctrine of predestination that could disempower and cause some adherents to lose a sense of their own free will. Thus, skeptics might consider astrology incompatible with the aims and methods of therapy. That can sometimes be a valid critique, as there are astrologers who speak in a fatalistic manner about planetary influences such as the negative effects of eclipses or various planetary debilitations, and they often end up instilling fear in others. That's why I emphasize the importance of using this knowledge in a way that empowers the person, clarifies key tasks, and identifies specific action plans; our work is to facilitate transformation at critical phases of life.

Therapeutic astrology interprets the planets psychologically, as representations of our varied human drives, motivations, and activities, such as feeling (Moon), thinking (Mercury), relating (Venus), asserting (Mars), planning (Jupiter), working (Saturn), and reorganizing (Uranus). We relate what is happening in the sky to what is happening inside us, within the human psyche. Analysis of the birth chart is a way to know oneself more clearly and objectively, to clarify a person's primary interests, motivations, and personality traits. It helps us understand spousal and family and business relationships and shows how people are organized differently from one another, so we can accept and love one another more deeply. Astrologers believe that our state of wellbeing and mental health can be positively affected through a trained attunement to nature's cycles and phases, indicated by celestial patterns. We observe correlations between cycles of planets and the developmental stages within a human lifetime. We strengthen the individual's creative will and give it an archetypally nuanced focus.

Astrology can help us track the natural fluctuations in mood and energy states that everyone experiences, to understand the specific challenges or suffering that can engender psychological distress, depression, or disorder, and to find a clear direction for the future so we can begin to do something positive to improve our situation. Psychotherapy integrating astrological symbolism to identify pressing issues and concerns can be clinically sound as well as immensely catalytic; I detailed many case examples in *Planets in Therapy*.[10]

Personally, I'm not in favor of using astrology to try to diagnose specific psychological disorders. I feel that's problematic because there's so much variation in how people respond to planetary placements and energies. I don't believe there's one astrological signature indicating paranoia, bipolar disorder, depression, schizophrenia, sociopathic personality disorders, and so forth. Nonetheless, we observe how particular symptoms and problems sometimes emerge as expressions of certain natal or transiting planets, for example, Mars: anger, discordant relationships, sexual problems and fixations; Saturn: depression, rigidity, fear of change; Uranus: agitation or mania, defiance, irresponsible behaviors; Neptune: denial, delusional thinking, addictions, relational victimization; Pluto: paranoia, domineering traits, violent outbursts, post-traumatic stress disorder. Astrological knowledge may be used to modify dysfunctional traits and behavioral patterns, refine the personality and improve a person's state of emotional and mental health. The proof of astrology's validity is ultimately found in the successful adaptation to life demonstrated by those who study and practice its core principles.

Certainly there are people who aren't psychologically sound enough to use astrology, who have an external locus of control and think things just happen to them and they have no volition. Then astrology is counterproductive and contraindicated. All medicines are contraindicated for some individuals. We're not saying this is right for everyone. It's not appropriate for someone in the grips of an active psychosis, or someone who uses astrology to abrogate responsibility and to feel disempowered and victimized by fate and destiny. No competent practitioner would support that attitude. A person needs the intellectual capacity to distinguish literal interpretation of planetary influence from metaphorical and poetic interpretation—to distinguish a symbol from a concrete reality. Rather than fearing the planets as forces that strictly determine what happens to us, we can approach the symbolism of the natal chart as an archetypally-themed structure that lends organization to our life planning and choices.

Astrology isn't a panacea that in itself will cure people of depression and anxiety disorders. It is knowledge that must be deeply studied and contemplated—and then acted upon. We discern in its symbolism images of the most favorable action to undertake at any moment. It inspires us to undertake life-transforming projects with a sense that this is the shape of things; this is the way things want to happen. This knowledge teaches us to live in accordance with our own true nature and to move with the rhythm of planetary cycles through various stages of life, informed by a unique time perspective that isn't found in any other discipline or field of study.

Transformative Chart Interpretation

Whether reading a chart for myself, a client, or a friend, as an astrologer I engage in a ritual act of establishing a center, a point of consciousness, a still point that observes the stream of endless change. In conducting sessions, my philosophy is to keep it simple. I try not to overwhelm clients (and myself) with too much information, too many techniques. I've pared down my methodology to analysis of the birth chart and transits, secondary progressions, and solar arc directions. This provides all the information I need. For my own chart I add midpoints, minor progressions, and tertiary progressions. With clients I stay with what I can easily explain and articulate: the natal chart and its aspects, transits, and progressions. Like most astrologers, I explore sign, house placement, and aspects of the Sun and Moon as these inform us about the person's identity and emotional demeanor. From these basic elements of the chart I start to discern recurrent issues and complexes, and how key events in a person's life are scripted in accordance with archetypal structures.

I like to start chart readings with a brief explanation of chart symbols, beginning with planets and signs. I want the client to gain a sense of how the chart represents the full range and complexity of their life-world. I explain how astrology describes (and encompasses) the wholeness of life, for example, the cycle of evolution signified by the zodiacal signs. Each practitioner translates astrology in line with our personal interests and background—for example, business and finance, politics, celebrities and entertainment, or human relationships. I became a student of yoga when I was 14 and I've always approached astrology as a form of yoga, a practice of self-unification through awareness of time and life cycles. Thus, I interpret the zodiacal signs as signifiers of twelve facets or phases of evolution, twelve central human concerns, and

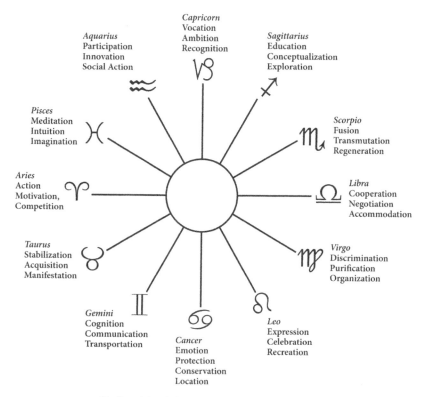

Zodiac Mandala: 12 Phases of Evolution

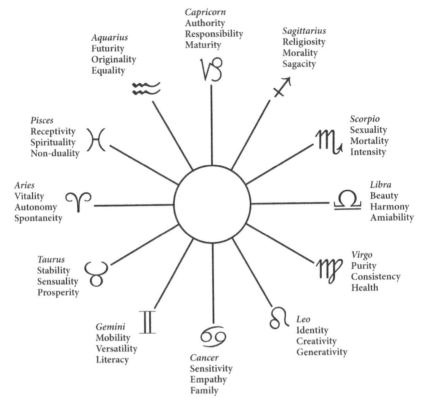

Zodiac Mandala: Central Human Concerns

twelve pathways to transformation. Figures 1, 2, and 3 show examples of a few evocative terms I might use to succinctly discuss the signs and the contrasts and interchange between them. I try to phrase things in a way that's a little different from traditional or stereotypical keywords. These themes are frequent points of discussion as we explore the horoscope's planetary placements in zodiacal signs.[11]

I typically focus on tracking Saturn's transits through the houses, noting time periods of Saturn's key aspects to natal planets and horoscope angles. From this I gain a better knowledge of the person's experiences and areas of concern. I always state that the purpose of the reading isn't to predict specific events but to gain a sense of orientation in time. From that orientation, we evoke images of what's possible, and also outline a series of steps, phases, and passages to get there.

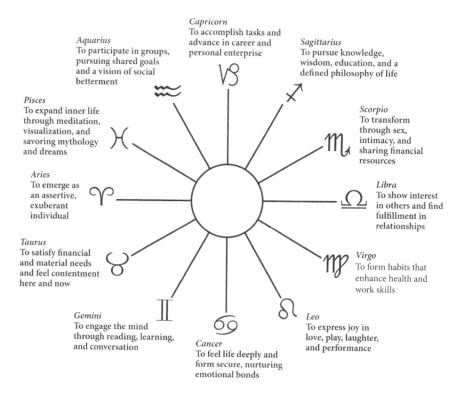

Capricorn
To accomplish tasks and advance in career and personal enterprise

Aquarius
To participate in groups, pursuing shared goals and a vision of social betterment

Sagittarius
To pursue knowledge, wisdom, education, and a defined philosophy of life

Pisces
To expand inner life through meditation, visualization, and savoring mythology and dreams

Scorpio
To transform through sex, intimacy, and sharing financial resources

Aries
To emerge as an assertive, exuberant individual

Libra
To show interest in others and find fulfillment in relationships

Taurus
To satisfy financial and material needs and feel contentment here and now

Virgo
To form habits that enhance health and work skills

Gemini
To engage the mind through reading, learning, and conversation

Leo
To express joy in love, play, laughter, and performance

Cancer
To feel life deeply and form secure, nurturing emotional bonds

Zodiac Mandala: 12 Yogas of the Zodiac

Dialogical Focus

Therapeutic astrology, as I understand it, is *dialogical, developmental*, and *process-oriented*. First and foremost, transformative readings emerge from dialogue, from posing questions. After explaining the general planetary symbolism, I'll ask the client questions such as: How do you express your Mars in the 9th house, or your stellium in Leo? How do 8th house themes manifest in your life? What happened in 1993 when Uranus and Neptune were conjunct your Sun? These questions allow the person to tell their story and show me how the chart is resonating, and whether its potentials are asleep or awakening. Rather than giving chart readings that are droning monologues, approaching the work as dialogue makes sessions lively and engaged. Our interpretation evolves as we learn the details of a person's life. The process also

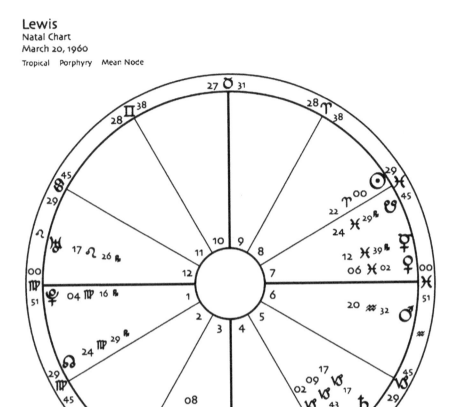

Lewis
Natal Chart
March 20, 1960
Tropical   Porphyry   Mean Node

involves dialogue with the planets themselves, meditating and considering, what does this planet want? How can I best express it?

For example, my client Lewis has Moon conjunct Jupiter-Saturn in Capricorn in the 5th house, and is well adapted to his social role and responsibilities as father of three children (5th house emphasis), and as sole owner of a manufacturing business. Ascendant ruler Mercury is conjunct Venus, dispositor of the Taurus Midheaven, symbolism suggesting the material focus of his enterprise, which involves working with factories, shipping and receiving, fulfilling orders, and interfacing with buyers from major retail chains. A series of consultations occurred during a three-time transit of Jupiter in Scorpio square natal Mars in the 6th house of employees and the workplace. Simultaneously, transiting Saturn made a three-time pass over 5° Capricorn, forming a semisquare to natal Mars at 20° Aquarius. When I spoke in general terms about possible stresses in the workplace that might coincide with these contacts to Mars, Lewis said he was having trouble with his director of sales and marketing, who was not performing up to expectations. But he would not fire the man, partly because he was afraid of the employee's anger and sometimes unpleasant demeanor (6th house Mars).

During one discussion we inquired, what does your Mars want right now? In what ways could Lewis exercise more initiative? Spontaneously he reported a recent dream featuring a man with slicked-back hair and wearing shiny, pointy loafers. Lewis said it reminded him of some guy he might meet in a casino, maybe a seedy character but also perhaps a shrewd and successful business entrepreneur. He decided that he would call him The Shark, someone who knows how to survive in the world and even sometimes to be the aggressor, the top fish on the food chain. He was definitely someone who looked out for his own best interests. Lewis told me that he realized he needed to be The Shark and fire his sales manager—to take a gamble and trust that this was the right move. He realized that he needed to do what's best for the business and for himself. This example illustrates how through reflective dialogue we start to relate to each planet as a living presence and a representation of our own potentials and faculties.

Developmental Emphasis

Therapeutic astrology is inherently developmental because it describes our movement through time and suggests paths to developing various faculties and facets of the self. We begin with the assumption that we can learn to evolve our expression of each planet, our embodiment of each archetype.

Consider Wayne's chart. He has Sun-Mercury in Gemini, along

with Saturn, Venus, and Moon conjunct his Gemini Ascendant, quincunx Jupiter and Neptune. Wayne reported that he was bored at work
and had started drinking cocktails at lunchtime and nipping on a flask
hidden in his desk at the office. At this time, transiting Uranus in
Pisces and Saturn in Virgo were both squaring his natal Sun-Mercury.
Transits to Mercury highlight tasks of learning and communication,
a need for stimulation, and an urge to evolve our thinking and communication skills. I pointed out that Wayne had the chart symbolism
of someone who could be drawn to writing, discussing ideas, and telling stories (Gemini emphasis). Wayne enjoyed reading fiction and he
started taking writing classes and working on short stories and then a
novel. Thereafter he changed his mindset, focused on his literary interests, and stopped drinking at work, and eventually stopped altogether.
He found that awakening an inner life of the imagination was more
satisfying than a life of alcoholism; he reached a higher expression of
his Sun-Neptune aspect. Alignment with the birth pattern releases our
natural vitality so we feel less depressed and less need to numb ourselves.
Wayne began to emanate the intelligence and observant wit of Mercury,
and the warmth of the Sun. He underwent a transformation of identity
(Uranus square Sun). Wayne acknowledges that doing this work isn't
all about becoming a famous writer, which is probably unlikely, but he
chooses to invest himself in this creative process because it's fun. It gives
him energy and motivation; it lights him up. He loves being part of the
game of reading and creating fiction. Awakening the Sun is the root of
good mental health because it represents confident emanation of one's
identity, and a feeling of dignity and healthy pride in myself, in who I
am—joy in being myself.

Now, nearly a decade later, Wayne actively studies literature and
creative writing and attends writers' groups. He has discovered that the
path is the goal and he enjoys being on that path. The astrologer's work
is to present a vision of potential that invites action and forward movement. Wayne continues to hold various jobs involving data processing
and retail management (five planets in Gemini, including Saturn in
Gemini), which provides needed economic sustainment. With Jupi-

Wayne
Natal Chart
June 21, 1971
Tropical   Koch   Mean Node

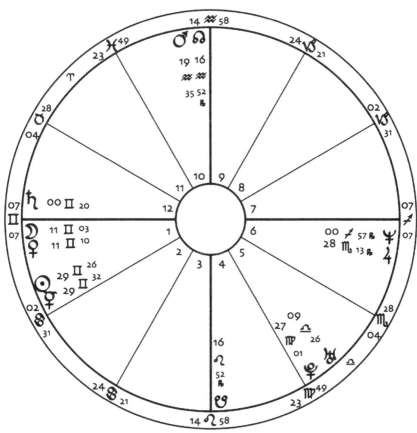

ter and Neptune at the Descendant, he enjoys learning about famous writers, befriends mystics and intellectuals, and is fascinated by the lives and thinking of great teachers and philosophers. He's an interesting and well-read man, a journeyman with multiple interests and work skills. Part of the development implicit in his chart's 1st house Sun-Mercury (trine Mars) is the need to be happy being himself—something of a character, observant, sarcastic, and, at his best, an engaging raconteur.

Process Orientation in Therapeutic Astrology

Therapeutic astrology is process-oriented and emphasizes meditating on chart symbols and actively striving to unfold the potentials indicated by the planets.[12] This approach helps us think about difficult life problems in new ways and work things through to reach deeper realizations of meaning. For example, my client Eileen told me she was depressed after breaking off a relationship with a man named Vincent. She said, "He didn't bring added value to my life. He wanted it to be all about me, in that he was completely devoted to me, but it was too

Eileen
Natal Chart
August 8, 1949
Tropical   Porphyry   Mean Node

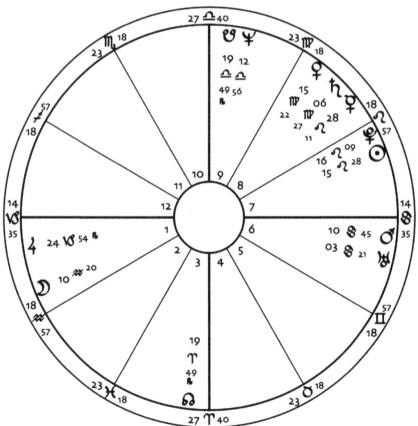

much for me. I felt smothered. I introduced him to new places, and to culture he'd never been exposed to, but what was I getting out of it?"

Many people would like to have someone devotedly paying attention to them, yet Eileen thought breaking up was the right decision. But she was plagued by doubts and wondering if she'd made a mistake. She turned to astrology to make sense of the situation, an answer to the question, was she doing the right thing? With natal Mars-Uranus in Cancer near the Descendant, her relationships had always been highly volatile, and emotionally intense, with a history of domestic quarrels and aggressive behavior. Eileen told me she was scared of men showing anger and strong emotion, and said, "I don't like it when a man is needy. For years I've been taking care of my mom; she's now almost 100 percent dependent on me. So I can't tolerate when a man expresses that he needs me. And I always seem to attract this type of clingy, needy man." I explained that Cancer represents the experience of attachment and mutual dependency. Mars in Cancer indicates that attachment is intense and stresses her with its longing for closeness and demand for contact comfort. I suggested that maybe she could learn to better tolerate normal attachment-seeking behaviors in her partner. But I wondered if this might touch a sensitive zone for her because Mars in Cancer can denote an emotionally volatile family matrix. Eileen replied, "My mom was always angry at dad. She mishandled the relationship, she was out of control, constantly enraged."

With north node in Aries (ruled by Mars) in the 3rd house, a lot of family stress focused on her sister Tess, whom Eileen described as mentally unstable, with severe OCD and anxiety. "There was always fighting between my sister and my mom. Tess was hysterical and screaming. Father left us and I think it had to be partly to get away from my sister."

I commented, "When a man gets close to you and begins to need you and wants to form an attachment with you, it feels very clingy and it touches your fear of the volatile emotionality of your sister. It makes you want to get away and withdraw. So you become the abandoning father." "Yes," she replied. "I identify with my father." This interpretation was spontaneous, not premeditated, arising organically within the conversation.

Look at Neptune's prominent place in Eileen's horoscope, ruling the 3rd house of siblings, and the most elevated planet, square the Ascendant, conjunct the south node. She was into meditation but also experienced sorrows, emptiness, and emotional numbness after she cut off the emotional connection and sexual pleasure and excitement that was available with Vince (Mars-Uranus setting). About two years later, Eileen called to consult me about a different relationship, with someone named Ron, and the story was exactly the same. She experienced him as clingy, needy, overly dependent on her, and intensely irritating. This relationship began when her progressed Moon in Cancer was conjunct her natal Mars and Descendant. Ron had Sun-Venus in Aquarius, exactly conjunct Eileen's Moon, symbol of a beautiful, loving, affectionate connection—potentially a love that's precious and rare. There was a strong mutual attraction, but Eileen had the same feelings come up as before. She wanted to flee because Ron wasn't sufficiently independent. He constantly expressed his passionate attraction to her, and then he was wounded and angry when she rejected him. It was helpful that I'd kept notes on our previous session so we could resume our conversation right where we'd left off. Eileen was now able to recognize that her problem wasn't that all the men in her life were defective. She was living out a pattern or psychological complex that shaped her experience of relationships.

Astrology gives us a highly nuanced understanding of our inner psychodynamics. Mars-Uranus in Cancer describes the way she organizes relationships. I said it would be hard to deny or completely negate the active, insistent effort of others—such as Ron and Vincent before him—to seek a strong emotional and physical attachment with her. She'd managed to tolerate living with her first husband for more than 20 years, so she was clearly capable of sustained intimacy. Ultimately, Eileen has to choose whether or not she can be in this relationship. She told me she didn't want to just keep breaking up again and again. And she said, "What we talked about regarding my sister—that really got to me."

Ron lived in a different part of the state and they lived apart, so Eileen thought that was another reason it was an impossible situation and could never work out. But I felt myself inwardly nudged by spirit or by my own intuition to gently disagree with her that it was a hopeless situation. I kept thinking about Ron's Sun-Venus conjunct her Moon and how fundamentally he must love her. As an astrologer, how can you ignore something like that? And it occurred to me that having some distance and independence from one another could actually work well for Eileen. At this point in life a traditional marriage wasn't import-ant to her. Maybe they could define their own agreement that included some degree of separation. That was the essence of the chart reading. In closing, I said that her chart emphasized the need to develop within both poles—autonomy and relatedness—balancing the 1st house Jupi-ter in Capricorn (a large, ambitious personality focused on her own professional advancement and need for independence) with the rela-tional energies signified by four planets in her 7th and 8th houses. I later learned that Eileen didn't break up with Ron; she stuck with him. He could be clingy at times, whiny, a little neurotic. They took turns coming to each other's houses. They had great sex, then returned to their respective domiciles; they had the best of both worlds. The last I heard, that's the state of their relationship.

Homage to Saturn: Organizing Your Life Astrologically

Another pillar of therapeutic astrology is the idea that this knowledge should aid us in practical spheres of life. Astrology is immensely use-ful in organizing our time, our actions and our life space, so we can coordinate activities in multiple realms simultaneously. It builds our effectiveness and helps us to develop a defined, crystalline organization that can cut through negativity, inertia, laziness, and the world's many distractions and forces of darkness so that we're in constant motion as a positive force in our world and able contributors in our various fields and enterprises.

I like to focus on getting organized at the level of Saturn, planet of maturation, social adaptation, and building resilient life structures. These tasks are emphasized at successive phases of Saturn's cycle. Astrologers who think in terms of gradual maturation over the course of an entire 30-year Saturn cycle, or over several Saturn cycles, gain a long-term view of life as an opus, a creative construction. Natal Saturn's position is the foundation that establishes a persistent life theme, while transiting Saturn presents challenges to reach specific milestones of development—for example, to pull our finances together when Saturn transits the 2nd house, or to secure and maintain a good place to live when Saturn is in the 4th; or to develop a deeper interior spiritual life when Saturn transits the 12th house.

Resourceful astrologers consciously engage in the structure-building processes and decisions that unfold through successive stages of the Saturn cycle. Saturn is the steady chronocrator that bestows opportunities to master various realms and life lessons. It stays in a sign and house long enough for us to get thoroughly familiar with the issues there, and hopefully to make some stabilizing improvements. Saturn is the rudder that helps us steer our ship through both calm and choppy waters, bringing order to chaos, through work and persistent effort. No matter what our lifepath, we reach the most beneficial outcomes by solving the challenges posed by Saturn.

In traditional astrology Saturn was viewed as a negative, malefic planet associated with suffering and adversities. Certainly it represents the reality principle, which forces us to encounter limits and cope with the aging process. However, for humanistic and psychological astrologers, Saturn is also signifier of the internal ordering, organizing principle. It represents responsibilities, life structures, and the work that's necessary for social adaptation and material stability. When I give chart readings, I try to help people meet the tests that Saturn poses for successful organization of life—material life, relational life, occupational life, intellectual life, spiritual life. We do this by describing in positive, constructive terms the requirements and responsibilities of Saturn.

Phil, age 48, had transiting Uranus in Aries conjunct his natal Saturn in Aries in the 8th house. He knew some astrology and was worried that Saturn in the 8th house meant he might die or there'd be some other death. My approach is to ask the client to breathe and consider what is the potential of this? What's the highest expression of this natal planet or this transit? I explained that the 8th house concerns interpersonal commitments and financial agreements, as well as issues about

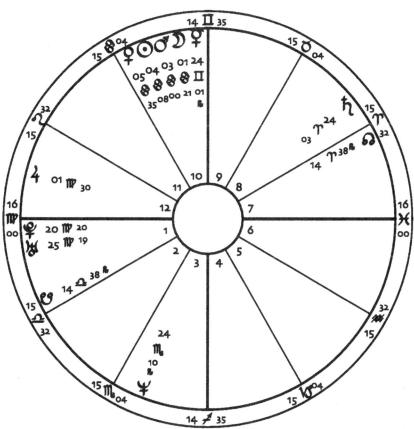

debt, credit, and taxes. Phil informed me that he was facing problems regarding repayment of student loans, credit card debts, and unpaid taxes—8th house issues. I conveyed to him that at this time some of his most important personal growth could occur by making changes in these areas (Uranus conjunct Saturn: major restructuring). Over the subsequent months Phil made considerable progress by calling the IRS and straightening out his taxes, paying off debts, and renegotiating his student loan repayment schedule. It was a process, not an event. It took about a year for him to get on an improved financial footing, and then things were much better. Even though this was expensive, Phil felt stronger and more inwardly serene because he knew where he stood and what his obligations were. That's positive transformation of Saturn. At the same time Phil was able to procure funding for a new business enterprise of his own: venture capital. Thus, he succeeded in the yoga of debt and taxes. Simultaneously, he and his girlfriend made plans to move in together and made shared financial commitments as they rented a house together. This occurred the week that transiting Saturn entered his 4th house, a major transit for establishing roots, home, and the structure of domestic life.

In chart readings I describe the need to embrace the tasks of Saturn's natal placement and its current transiting position: Saturn in the 3rd house: learning, reading, writing, and also driving or transportation, focusing on learning routes, how to get from place to place; Saturn in the 6th house: working on health issues and healthy habits and routines; gaining skills in the workplace, training employees or being trained in the workplace; Saturn in the 8th house: having financial responsibilities to others, investment and financial planning in marriage and business; Saturn in the 11th: engagement in group activity and commitments to organizations or social movements.

When I read a chart, I track the form-building and form-sustaining tasks of Saturn's cycle, the maturational Saturn transits we face every 7–8 years.[13] Saturn's transits through each house shows specific areas where we're working hard, experiencing pressure to commit, organize, and accomplish things, and hopefully becoming more grounded and self-disciplined. I know there are some astrologers who will tell clients that Saturn entering the 7th house is a malefic or unfavorable transit for love and friendships. But I prefer to tell the person that at this time Saturn presents tasks of maturation and intelligence about relationships.

Look at the chart of Daron, a successful screenplay writer in Hollywood who mainly works in the Sci Fi, fantasy, and horror genres. With his Sun-Mercury conjunction in Scorpio you see the writer, comfortable with gore, blood and creepy scenes, dealing with cryptic themes of death, spirits, monsters, vampires, and poltergeists. Sun squares its dispositor Pluto in the 4th house. His father was a mean, dominating alcoholic who violently assaulted his wife (Daron's mother) and Daron's older brother. A key theme of Daron's films is their depiction of families falling apart and families trying to heal and reconcile. He described to me the stress of working on multiple projects, deadlines, dealing with film management and producers, and trying to keep up as a writer in his mid-sixties in a culture and town that's youth-obsessed. Plus, with natal Saturn in the 5th house, his 15-year-old daughter is a ball of anxiety. Daron has had four marriages, four divorces, lots of

Daron
Natal Chart
November 8, 1949
Tropical   Porphyry   Mean Node

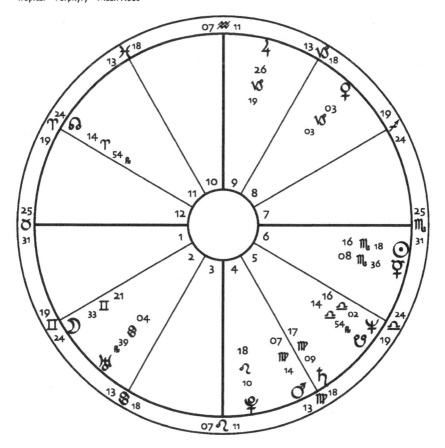

drugs, overdoses, car crashes, the full range of Sun square Pluto hellish underworld experiences, emergencies, endings, and crisis situations.

I asked Daron what had happened recently, when transiting Saturn in Scorpio was conjunct his Sun in Scorpio. That's a key method. Ask about recent transits of Saturn conjunct, opposite, or square natal planets and you'll immediately learn what's going on in the person's life.

Daron said, "My last wife had an affair. It was devastating. It took me down a long road with a lot of anger and jealousy." That sounds like Scorpio energy. At the time of our initial consultation, transiting Saturn was just entering his 7th house, a developmentally appropriate time to prioritize finding a stable relationship. He said, "I've been dating someone who has pulled back from me—Helen. She suffers from depression, and is afraid of commitment. She bolted. Now I feel empty and alone." I looked at Helen's chart, which Daron brought with him, and noted that Helen was not having any apparent strong relational energy in her current transits, so it wasn't surprising that she wasn't into it; she said she wanted to break up. But Daron continued to pursue her, even though it wasn't working between them. Over the course of several sessions I encouraged Daron to let Helen go, not just because of her chart but because she directly told him she wasn't ready for a serious relationship with him. Referring to the realism Saturn can instill in us, I said, "Why not take her statement at face value and be open to meeting somebody else who actually wants the type of connection you want, someone who says and feels inwardly that she's ready." As I looked in the ephemeris I saw the rhythm of the Saturn retrograde transit and I observed that over the next two months, as Saturn turned stationary direct in his 7th house, the process of creating a new relationship could reach a pivotal phase.

Soon thereafter, Daron went back on Match.com, and met someone who was eager to have a relationship, and they actually got married very quickly. They made the decision, consulted with me about the best day to proceed, and they went to the courthouse to tie the knot. Of course I picked a day with Moon conjunct Venus, which I always prefer when electing a marriage date. It happened to be the following day, but they were immediately on it! They really wanted this and they went for it. By following Saturn's passages through the houses, we can steer our lives and create structures that are resilient, viable, and suitable. We study the person's present adaptation to life and try to enhance it.

Life Review Through Tracking the Saturn Cycle

To further illustrate how I use Saturn's transit cycle to revision the life story and to gently heal, let's consider the story of Judith, in her mid-fifties, who was suffering from major depression. A series of sessions that focused on the transits of Saturn enabled her to recall and inwardly resolve some pivotal events that had emotionally injured her. Judith came from a family that belonged to an evangelical church. Natal Saturn-Neptune were conjunct the midheaven, forming a T-square to natal Mars in Capricorn in the 1st house and square Uranus in Cancer in the 7th house. In high school, at her first Saturn opposition, she became very attractive to young men; but her father was uncomfortable about her budding sexuality and tried to shame her and told her to resist and suppress her instinctual desires. Transiting Saturn was in the 4th house of family, square natal Mars. You immediately get the feeling of her natal Saturn square Mars and square Uranus, and the tension these aspects imply. Judith rebelled and dated different boys, including several who were not members of their church community, causing heated family controversy (Mars opposite Uranus in Cancer). At age 21, Judith relented to her parents' wishes and married another church member, as Saturn transited through Cancer in her 7th house, but they immediately started quarreling, and she soon discovered that her husband was weird and inflexible (Uranus in the 7th). They were emotionally incompatible, and Judith became quite disillusioned (transiting Saturn square natal Saturn and Neptune in Libra). By her first Saturn return, she was experiencing serious marriage problems and domestic violence (Saturn in Libra square Mars and Uranus). Sadly, her husband struck her for being disobedient (Mars in 1st house: assault against her person and her body). However, family and members of her community told her she just had to bear it, that this was her cross to bear as a devoted wife. Their religion doesn't condone divorce and it's grounds for excommunication from the Church. Note how Saturn-Neptune

Judith
Natal Chart
November 4, 1952
Tropical   Porphyry   Mean Node

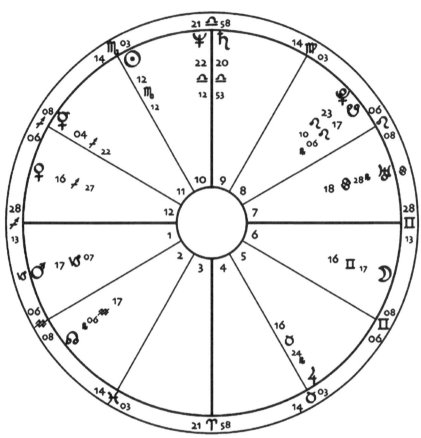

signifies a devout religious family, but also the possibility of being in denial.

When Judith finally had the courage to file for a divorce her entire community shunned her. This occurred when Saturn in Scorpio was conjunct her Sun in the 11th house. She encountered viciousness within the group, rather than love and support. Instead of standing by her and condemning her husband's abusive conduct, everyone took his side and rejected her. Transiting Pluto also passed through early Scorpio in the mid 1980s and passed over her natal Sun in the 11th house, representing unpleasantness and painful exile from her community. No one would speak to Judith and they treated her as if she were already dead. In a sense, the central meaning of Judith's life thus far was contained in transiting Pluto conjunct her Sun: facing evil; feeling betrayed and shunned by everyone she loved; feeling minimized as a person and reduced to nothing. She was traumatized. But astrology helped her pass through an emotional rebirth by touching these original wounds and core traumas, and clarifying how her life was manifesting a coherent series of archetypal structures and experiences.

All of this had occurred about 25 years earlier, but the impact on Judith's wellbeing had been devastating. She was severely depressed, living a solitary existence, and eating a very unhealthy diet that included periodic binges of over-eating, as a compensation for her many unfulfilled emotional needs. At the time of our initial consultation, transiting Saturn was in Virgo, square her natal Moon in the 6th house. I explained to Judith that Moon represents mother, and the archetypal experience of being held and cared for, and also the process of becoming one's own mother, caring for oneself, as well as caring for others. The fact that her own mother had rejected her after the divorce had been a source of profound grief. Moon carries our emotional memory. When someone comes for a horoscope reading at the time of a major transit to the Moon you have the opportunity to touch upon some of the most sensitive, important feelings and memories a person is carrying. The natal Moon's sign and house position indicates an emotionally laden zone of the horoscope and life-world, something we care about deeply. Judith was quite bored at her job (Gemini Moon in 6th). I suggested that perhaps she could develop an interest in issues and skills that might help her advance in her workplace; she decided to take some coursework in data sciences. She truly cared about her coworkers and enjoyed interesting conversations and close emotional connections with some of the women in the workplace, which made it feel like a good place to be. Judith was also becoming aware of deep sadness about becoming estranged from her children after the divorce and her banishment from their community.

As astrologers it's important that we employ some sensitive interpretive nuance. Some would simply say that the native is likely to feel depressed during transiting Saturn square the Moon. But using a developmental, process-oriented approach we can frame it differently. I told Judith that Saturn squaring her natal Moon was an opportune time to find new ways to satisfy her basic needs and gain more emotional strength and inner security. Certainly this transit indicated the importance of the hard work she was doing in psychotherapy. Judith realized that she wanted to clean and reorganize her cluttered living space, and she imagined herself sitting down to some nourishing meals and then actually began to do this while retrograde Saturn squared her Moon again. By the time Saturn turned direct in motion, squaring her natal Moon, she reconnected with her children, now young adults, who, she discovered, very much needed to connect with their mother. Judith evolved beyond a state of inert depression by developing her Moon, her capacity to feel and digest core events and painful memories of the past, while also developing stronger, more nurturing emotional attachments in the present time.

During her second Saturn return over the next two years, with Saturn in Libra, square natal Mars and Uranus, Judith became romantically involved with a woman. She got to experience more of her passionate, sexual Mars quincunx Pluto in the 8th house, and enjoyed the exciting, socially controversial energies suggested by Mars opposite Uranus in her 7th house. This example shows how astrology promotes emotional repair and maturation, self-liberation and individuation, living the totality of one's potentials, and reconciling the opposites, including masculine-feminine, and spirituality and sexuality (Mars and Neptune).

Transits, Progressions, and the Narrative Function of Astrology

The last example, the story of Judith, demonstrated what I call the narrative function of astrology, by which I mean that it's a way to organize our understanding of a person's biography and serves as a way to reconfigure our telling of the life story. As psychologist Donald Polkinghorne explained:

Narrative is one of the forms of expressiveness through which life events are conjoined into coherent, meaningful, unified themes.... [A narrative is] a linked series of episodes contributing to a single adventure with a beginning, middle, and an end.... We achieve our personal identity and self concept through the use of the narrative configuration, and make our existence into a whole by understanding it as an expression of a single unfolding and developing story.... The self is that temporal order of human existence whose story begins with birth, has as its middle the episodes of a life span, and ends with death. It is the plot that gathers together these events into a coherent and meaningful unity, and thereby gives context and significance to the contribution that individual episodes make toward the overall configuration that is the person.[14]

Astrologers employ a narrative sensibility by identifying unified life themes (evident in the natal pattern) and distinct episodes (linked to transits and progressions) that comprise moments in a larger unfolding story, a larger cycle of existence that encompasses the lifespan. Taking our point of departure from the birth chart symbolism, astrologers plot out a series of events that are shown to have an underlying cohesion, which clarifies the nature of the person we've become and are in the process of becoming.

In narrative approaches to counseling and psychotherapy we narrate or tell a story about our past and present life and construct the story of the future. This includes discovery of the identity and attitudes of the narrating *agent*, description of the *settings* or environments where the story occurs, which might include the home, school, the workplace, a journey or travel destination; and acknowledgment of the influences of important people such as family, friends, spouse, coworkers, adversaries, and mentors—the *characters* in our story. The story shows, or anticipates, the results of *actions* taken, or not taken, to reach *goals* that will satisfy our needs, and *instruments* utilized to reach goals, such as our abilities, friends, family, or employers. The story includes moments of decision and indecision or wavering, moments of accelerated activity, and pauses in the flow of events.[15]

Therapeutic astrological counseling is a process of listening to the person's story and using planetary cycles and symbols to sort out the most significant details, recurring themes, and chapters of the life that are central to understanding identity, how the person sees himself or herself, the choices available, hindrances and impediments, and future plans or desires. We compose a life history that articulates a sense of a life problem or a life mission. Counseling clarifies the gap between what the current situation is and what the person wants it to be, and what the person can do about that—what actions or adjustments are needed. The focus is on changing life structures, identifying projects, enacting roles, trying out activities, crystalizing decisions, and making commitments that shape the future life story.[16] Think of how Eileen (earlier in this chapter) came to recognize the recurring story of her relationships where she felt suffocated by clingy, needy people, and then she was able to create a new story in which she could have a healthy relationship that wasn't a traditional marriage or cohabiting relationship.

Astrology has the power to reorganize our understanding of past events and the meaning of crucial phases of the life we've already lived. In the next example, a simple comment at the beginning of a chart reading opened floodgates of feeling and took us to the very beginning of the story that defined a person's identity. Therapeutic astrology makes possible a more intensely felt emotional experience of one's life as a whole.

Alice, age 43, had Sun in the 12th house in Leo and Saturn in late Cancer. I began the chart reading by noting that at age 1–2 Saturn transited over her natal Sun. That struck me as significant. I asked Alice if she'd been hospitalized or isolated in some way at that age. Alice replied that when she was one year old her parents left her in the care of a relative and she didn't see them again for two years. She felt completely abandoned by her parents and she'd never been able to understand why. She teared up talking about this and said, "My entire life has been affected by this." She'd always felt quietly hurt that she hadn't been important to her parents, and that they had left her. It was an injury to the self, an experience that had been repeated many times in her friendships and love relationships. This original wound had also

Alice
Natal Chart
August 9, 1975
Tropical   Porphyry   Mean Node

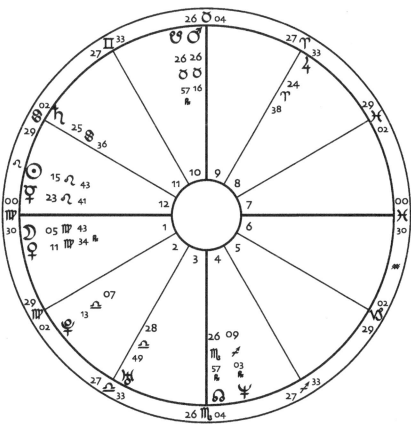

made her sensitive, spiritual, introspective, and compassionate toward those who suffered and were alone. It was no accident that she grew up to become a social worker who worked with homeless children, orphans, and refugees (12th house Sun in Leo: altruistic activity in the service of children). My comment about Saturn transiting her Sun at age 1–2 was nearly the first thing I said about her chart and our conversation went to a place of emotional depth in about five minutes. We instantly touched the wound to the Sun and the heart of Alice's longing to be seen and acknowledged by others.

In therapeutic astrology we revision the meaning of past events so we're able to shed old baggage and move on with our lives, more at peace with ourselves. It's thus a means to achieve *ego integrity*, which, as Erik Erikson described it, is the acceptance of one's past choices and outcomes, and the capacity to forgive oneself, to be reconciled with oneself, and accept the life one has lived, including mistakes, releasing the burden of regrets. Ego integrity is the ability to gaze back at past events and choices with wisdom, humor, and compassion. As the astrologer-sage Dane Rudhyar taught, astrologers situate events within the context of larger cyclic processes,[17] and I believe this greatly strengthens the feeling of ego integrity.

A woman's marriage ended during a long transit of Pluto through her 7th house; a lot of unpleasantness and negativity emerged between Sheila and her husband, Brian. Sometimes their lesser angels took hold of them as they erupted into furious arguments. Sheila didn't recognize her husband as the same person, he felt so hostile and contemptuous, so fundamentally armored and shut down. It was helpful for her to understand this change in their marriage in light of the archetype of Pluto. During that time Brian became, in her eyes, an incarnation of the death lord, Hades, god of the underworld. By association, she imagined herself as the maiden Persephone forced into bondage to her husband, lover, and master. Through this timeless symbolism, she mythologized the latter period of this marriage as her time of captivity in the underworld, constantly facing his anger, resentment, and need for absolute control. And just as Persephone was released from the underworld, the divorce was her emancipation. Knowledge of that long Pluto transit didn't mitigate the sad reality that their marriage ended, but it validated Sheila's feeling of finality, closure and a defined ending. She came to understand that their karma as a couple was clearly exhausted, so she could move on and stop berating herself and feeling ashamed about her divorce. From that point forward Sheila felt released from bondage and ready to begin a new life. Pluto's endings mark a branching of our life path in a new direction. Leaves and branches die, but the tree climbs on. This is an example of how the narrative function of astrology operates.

Using the timing methods of transits and progressions, we can identify key phases of life already experienced and we can imagine and visualize the future life we'd like to manifest. Transits indicate how environmental pressures activate the potentials and personality structures shown by the natal chart. For more on this, see the detailed tutorial on transits in *Planets in Therapy*. Many astrologers also use the method of *secondary progressions*, which show how our personality structures evolve slowly from within, discerned by studying planetary movements and aspects in the days following our birth and how these signify developments in corresponding years of the individual's life. Secondary progressions, based on the formula *one day after birth equals one year of life*, measure structural changes occurring within the birth pattern and the internal life-world. Progressions are especially useful for reconstructing key phases and facets of our life narrative. I pay special attention to the sign, house, and aspects of the progressed Sun and Moon, and also track aspects of progressed Mercury, Venus, and Mars.[18]

Transits and progressions portray stages in personality unfoldment over time, and generate many retrospective insights. In the next example I interpret some key events and features of a man's life narrative through assessment of the progressed chart.

Let's consider the chart of Eddie (also discussed in Chapter 5). With his 6th house stellium, Eddie is very involved in his occupational role and supervises many employees as a corporate manager. Natal Venus was approaching conjunction with the Sun, and his progressed Sun-Venus conjunction became exact in high school, where he met his girlfriend, Tanya. A Sun-Venus conjunction often signifies a time for love. As progressed Sun-Venus-Saturn came into conjunction he developed this relationship and married Tanya at age 20, with his progressed Moon also in Libra, sign of partnership. Simultaneously, progressed Mars was conjunct natal Moon: His mother strongly disapproved of Tanya, who apparently drank too much, used vulgar language, and berated Eddie in constant domestic quarrels. Progressed Mars was conjunct Moon for several years, and Eddie had ongoing problems with both his mother and his wife. With progressed Sun-Venus-Saturn, he felt responsible for Tanya and married her partly out of obligation. In

1990–91, his Saturn return occurred during a transiting Jupiter-Saturn opposition, with Saturn conjunct his Sun, Moon, Mercury, Saturn; at that time, he was promoted up the ranks in the workplace (6th house). Progressed Mars was conjunct Mercury; he was quarreling with his wife. Then progressed Mars came into conjunction with Saturn for several years, and Tanya made life intolerable, and wouldn't let him rest. They had a very abusive marriage and Tanya hit him repeatedly. He never struck her and endured her fury, showing a high degree of self-control,

Eddie
Natal Chart
January 6, 1962
Tropical   Porphyry   Mean Node

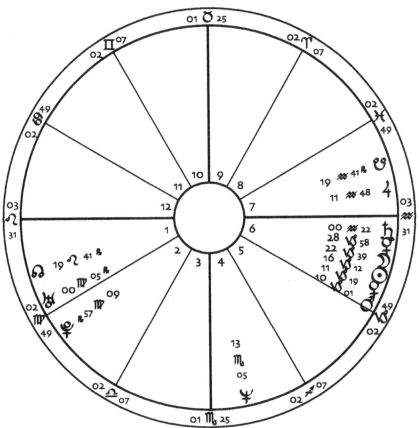

even under the stress of Mars conjunct natal Saturn. During these years when progressed Mars-Saturn were conjunct at, or near, his descendant degree, his progressed Sun-Venus-Jupiter were conjunct in Aquarius: Tanya spent a lot of money, wanted luxury, clothes, jewelry, a huge house. At the same time, Eddie met his future second wife, Sita. At this point they were just very close friends. Eddie has natal Jupiter in the 7th house. Sita is tall, a teacher and wise woman. She steadies him.

In 2006–7 Eddie had his progressed Full Moon at 29° Leo/Aquarius and Moon then entered Virgo, conjunct Uranus and Pluto in Virgo. One would expect a crisis. He contracted Lyme's disease, causing physical discomfort and disruption of his work and employment, and the treatment cost a great deal of money. At his progressed Full Moon, the Sun was at his 8th house cusp (debt), opposite Moon in Virgo, conjunct Uranus-Pluto in Gemini: Sally sued for divorce and took everything: the house, fancy car, and all the money. Eddie made an adaptive response by letting go and starting over, shedding possessions and resentments, partnering with Sita, his beloved spiritual soul sister. They have a very close marriage and have been together for a number of years now.

From the perspective of astrology, we have to live through the storms, and exhaust our karma with dispassion. Even when life delivers us some form of unhappiness, we have a framework and symbolism to discern the timing and what it all means. This helps us acknowledge transitions, invite shifts of energy, and anticipate new possibilities. It took about one hour of interpretation and conversation to learn all of this and to organize a new understanding of Eddie's life narrative. That's the power of the progressed chart.

Even though decades had passed since these events, Eddie still teared up speaking about how emotionally volatile this period was. It was comforting to realize that progressed Mars conjunct Moon and Saturn had been tumultuous, but it was in the past. One of the major storms in his life had already happened. Eddie was grateful to have survived that first marriage intact and to now be with a spouse with whom he was truly compatible.

Assessing Multiple Sources of Influence

Therapeutic astrologers are mindful of the importance of judicious and constructive use of language, free of determinism, in chart and transit interpretation. We emphasize maturational tasks, the exercise of free will, and the idea that the locus of change is ultimately within us. Of course, we also recognize sources of change that are seemingly outside of us, where we're subject to forces and events outside our control. Astrologers study how lives are shaped by ancestral and karmic forces (for example, through the lunar nodes), and by social trends and collective events keyed to transits (for example, the recent Uranus-Pluto square, which we'll discuss in Chapter 6). The perspective of astrology is that we can best determine our individual goals and intentions as we form a felt response to being part of a larger whole and a broader wave of human change.[19] We're also subject to influences that are *archetypal*, rooted in instinctual patterns of behavior common to human beings. These archetypal influences are inscribed in the natal pattern and manifest in response to transits. Astrology is a practice in which our free will is exercised within precisely scripted and organized structures— the archetypal forms and energies that are our principle focus in the next chapter.

Some powerful influences beyond the control of the individual emanate from the outer planets, Uranus, Neptune, and Pluto, which activate unconscious forces and sometimes trigger experiences in which we're turned upside down, and must cope and cooperate with change. An astrological perspective is particularly helpful in finding meaning at moments of ostensible defeat when the universe apparently has something much better in mind for us than what we want or expect; and we recognize this is the way life inexorably wants to happen.[20] Part of the value of astrology is that it teaches us that even in turbulent times, we can respond from an organized, cohesive center, a self, a formed identity symbolized by the natal Sun. That's what astrology can do for us; it helps us get ourselves organized. Guided by this celestial perspective, tumultuous changes and personal ordeals morph into conscious passages and initiations; we intuit the purpose of what is happening to us, the spiritual reason why this particular change is needed.

Julius, a music producer, had a falling out with his longtime business and creative partner, when transiting Pluto in Capricorn was quincunx his natal Leo Sun in the 7th house of partnership and friendship. His former collaborator Bernard had an egotistical outburst in which he expressed a lot of resentments and feelings of being slighted and insulted (Pluto aspecting Sun in Leo), and he made some extremely hostile and derogatory comments towards Julius. All of this poured out in a single incident of narcissistic rage. This marked the absolute end of a 20-year friendship, which was very painful. Julius said it felt

Julius
Natal Chart
August 12, 1969
Tropical   Koch   Mean Node

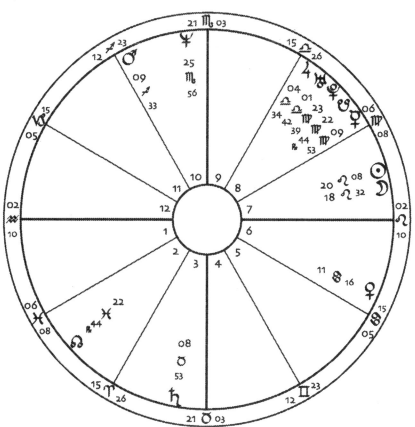

Julius
Reference Chart
Natal Chart
Tuesday, August 12, 1969

Current Transits
2nd Chart
Natal Chart
Friday, July 20, 2018
12:00:00 PM PDT
Berkeley, California

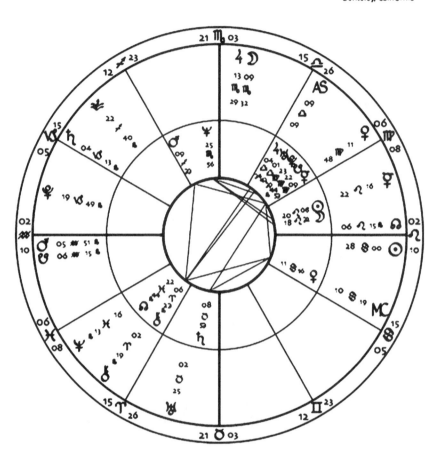

like a punch in the gut, which is apt because Sun rules the solar plexus chakra, *manipura*, the energetic center of one's personal esteem and self-confidence. He felt injured by Bernard's negation of all he (Julius) had done for him. Pluto's transit to his Sun brought a scorching burning of bridges, after everything that will ever be said between them was said, followed by a rupture, a termination, a cutting off of a branch. But this break ultimately caused Julius to seek out and commence collaborations with other musicians, leading to fresh sounds and new directions, marking a phase of creative and artistic rebirth. Simultaneously, transiting Uranus formed a square to his Ascendant, marking change, a break with the past, independence, going his own way.

The examples in this chapter illustrate some of the central themes and practices of therapeutic astrology. Now we turn to a hybrid technique that fully consummates the marriage between astrology and depth psychology.

CHAPTER 3

Jung, Astrology, and Dreams: Synchronicity and the Manifestation of Archetypes

One of my favorite approaches to therapeutic astrology is to combine our celestial art with dream interpretation. I evolved this method inspired by the work of C. G. Jung, whose writings captivated me as a teenager, when I read *The Portable Jung* from cover to cover. When I was in my early twenties going through my Neptunian meltdown, I practiced the methods he originated: recording dreams and interpreting them in a journal, doodling and drawing mandalas, working actively with symbols, consulting the I Ching as an oracle, and allowing the imagination free play. And Jung was the original psychological astrologer.

One way I've found to let the psyche breathe in the service of change is to study the profound connections between astrology and dreams, both areas of profound interest to Jung. In this chapter I describe a methodology that combines astrology with dream interpretation, practices that have always gone together for me—keeping dream journals while closely following transits. As a psychotherapist I note correlations between clients' dreams and what's going on for them astrologically. Combining astrology with Jungian dreamwork has immense healing power. Dream images often reflect the symbolism of natal or transiting planets, which in turn illuminates the meaning of dreams. Both dreams and astrology are expressions and manifestations of the deep unconscious and its core structures, its secret plan for our evolution. Both heighten our awareness of the guiding archetypes of the moment, so we can participate consciously in these eternal patterns of transformation. Dreams and astrology both offer fresh perspectives on the past, phases of life already lived, spotlighting pivotal events and traumas that need healing and resolution. Astrology and dreamwork are integrative, clarifying our current tasks, portraying our recurrent emotional states, core complexes, and subpersonalities that need to be reconciled and amalgamated to achieve wholeness. Astrology and dreams are also prospective and anticipatory, revealing what's emerging for us, and visions of what we can become.

Jung once said of dreams: "Every interpretation is a hypothesis, an attempt to read an unknown text."[21] He said the dream "shows the inner truth and reality of the patient as it really is, . . . not as he would like it to be, but as it is."[22] Jung taught that each dream compensates for the dreamer's conscious viewpoint or feelings and provides unexpected, alternative perceptions and viewpoints; and every dream can be considered a communication from our inner Self, guide and director of the individuation process, the urge to become what one is.[23] In a similar manner, the natal chart portrays us as we really are, and as the universe intends us to be; and every interpretation of a birth chart is a hypothesis, an attempt to read an unknown text, revealing the wisdom of a superior organizing intelligence.

In the future I believe the link between astrology and dreams will become a major focus of depth psychology. Of course, strong opposition to our doctrines still exists, and currently the deep freeze of astrology out of academic discourse remains in effect. Psychologists are generally wary of astrology, viewing it as a form of pseudoscience. Years ago, when I was turned down for admission to training to become a Jungian psychoanalyst, I was told it was largely because some members of the interviewing committee looked askance at my involvement with this field. This was surprising to me given their founder's enthusiastic interest in the subject. Jung was deeply immersed in study of esoteric knowledge, myth and mysticism, and was an avid astrologer who cast birth charts for many of his patients.[24]

Jung influenced our field in many ways. For example, he studied horoscopes of married couples to understand Sun-Moon contact between charts, to assess emotional compatibility, and to understand how people embodying opposing traits come to complete one another. This birthed the study of synastry and foreshadowed the work of Lois Sargent, Stephen Arroyo, and Ronald Davison showing how astrology is a basis for couples counseling, which has inspired my own work as a Marriage and Family Therapist.[25]

Also, Jung's model of the psyche's conscious and unconscious realms greatly expands the meaning we attribute to the 12th house as a realm of psychological gestation and experience of the unconscious through dreams, imagination, intuition, mythology, and discovery of the archetypal dimension. Through a Jungian lens, the transition from the 12th house to the Ascendant represents a psychological birth, comparable to the transition from Pisces to Aries. We begin in the Piscean state of oneness, the fish, the sea, a state of no-separation, nonduality, and innate wholeness. Movement into Aries and the 1st house is analogous to the emergence of the mythical ancestor or hero who encounters and vanquishes a dragon or sea monster (symbolizing the unconscious, the Pisces and 12th house realm), which represents differentiation of the ego, self-assertive drive, wielding the power of will and individual self-determination. For astrologers, this is every person's story, written into the structure of the horoscope, which depicts the timeless mythos of the hero or heroine seeking to differentiate and become a distinct individual, to individuate.

Jung's case studies showed how dreams promote individuation, the process of unfolding our uniqueness and the totality of who we are. This influenced Dane Rudhyar, originator of humanistic astrology, to formulate the idea that the astrological birth chart is a map of the individuation process, the process of unfolding our inborn potentials over the course of time, as we respond to various transits and challenges. Astrology and depth psychology are both ways to find our deep center and to discern the innate pattern or spiritual blueprint of personality— through study of the natal chart, and through analysis of dreams. And it's even more powerful to study astrology and dreams together. The practice of astrological dreamwork is like a potent serum that regenerates the psyche.

Archetypes and Planetary Symbolism

Jung viewed astrology primarily as a mythological language. He wrote, "Astrology, like the collective unconscious with which psychology is concerned, consists of symbolic configurations. The planets are the gods, symbols of the power of the unconscious."[26] For Jung, the archetypes of the collective unconscious signify archaic, typical, and recurrent features and patterns of human experience—birth and death, separation from parents, initiation, and marriage; recurrent figures such as the divine child, warrior, maiden and crone; shaman or wounded healer; the shadow, rival, or adversary; the beloved, which Jung personified as anima and animus; the savior or messiah; the outcast, bête noire, or scapegoat; mythical creatures such as the ouroboros; and archetypal animals such as snake, lion, fish, leopard, ostrich, monkey, and so forth. I described many examples of dreams with archetypal themes in *Dreamwork and Self-Healing*, and for this chapter I've included several dreams from that book that I'll discuss here in a very different context.

As explained by Robert Aziz, just as finches are born with an innate, instinctual fear of predatory birds, so too:

> in the psyches of human beings there . . . are innate patterns of behavior and meaning which . . . similarly become activated to facilitate human adaptation. . . . Jung observed and studied the spontaneous emergence of such patterns, which followed themes of universal significance such as dismemberment and renewal, wholeness and self-realization, the God-man, the hero, the mandala, initiatory ordeals and rites of passage, the great mother, death and rebirth, the wise old man, the hostile brothers, the birth of the hero, the trickster figure, and spiritual journeys of ascent and descent. . . .[27]

Psychologically-oriented astrologers view the planets as messengers or expressions of these formative archetypes, timeless patterns of transformation that shape our development over the lifespan. One could even define astrology as the discovery of archetypal meanings in every situation of life as we achieve synchrony with planetary movements. That synchrony is *wholeness*—the state of resonance with the order of the cosmos.

The birth chart represents how our evolution is organized by archetypal patterns. If you have the Moon rising, culminating, or in other prominent position you may find yourself often nurturing others and playing a mothering, supporting role, embodying the Moon-Mother archetype in your own way. That archetype recurs or becomes a constant in development.

Or let's say you have Jupiter rising, or aspecting Sun, or many planets in Sagittarius. Pursuing the path of the scholar, educator, priest, or philosopher is part of your archetypal makeup. This archetype of education, knowledge, and intellectual life may appear in, or be a key theme of dream images, especially at times of transits and progressions involving Jupiter or planets in Sagittarius. Once, when transiting Saturn conjoined my natal Jupiter, I had a vivid dream about the philosopher-sage Paul Ricoeur, from whom I'd once taken a course at University of Chicago, an exceptionally wise and brilliant man. In his natal chart Ricoeur has Jupiter rising in Capricorn, sextile natal Sun and Mercury, closely sesquare to Saturn. He embodied the Jupiterian philosopher archetype—a fully realized man of knowledge, and appearing as my dream character he represented that archetype within my own psyche and development.

Brian, a young man with Sun conjunct Jupiter in Leo, was in law school, training to become a prosecutor, a trial lawyer. He dreamed:

> *I am with a man and woman I know. We entered a cave opening and an underground cave system, which is partially flooded with water. There's no light in some places. Zeus is sleeping nearby in the back of the cave. He's in his robe and lying on his back. He doesn't get any prayers anymore so he's falling asleep. We go up a staircase next to him, with a torch guiding everyone out of the cave through a maze. No one knows the way out but me. We press on, turning corner after corner.*

The dream depicts a mythic journey into the depths of the unconscious, the watery cave, where, sleeping in his psyche, he meets Zeus, the Greek god of moral authority, reasoned judgment, righteousness and punishment of transgressors. That Jupiter–Zeus archetype is dor-

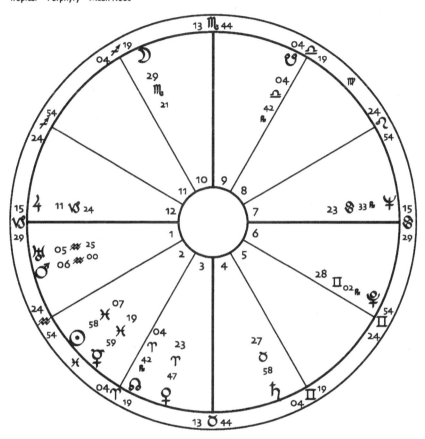

Paul Ricoeur
Natal Chart
February 27, 1913
4:00:00 AM GMT
Valence, France
44N56 / 4E54
Tropical Porphyry Mean Node

mant, sleeping; it is present and potentially awakening, influencing his present development. It was significant that in the dream Brian holds the torch and leads other people out of the darkness. His Sun-Jupiter signified a capacity for principled social and moral leadership, symbolized by Zeus.

An archetype (such as father, warrior, shaman, artist, priest, serpent) is not a dead concept. It's a living force, a yeasty, fermenting change principle. An archetype is one of the characteristic patterns or ways in which transformations happen. According to Anthony Stevens, "There exists in human beings certain psychic and behavioral forms which, while achieving unique expression in each individual, are, at the same time, universally present in all members of our species." [28] The archetypes are themes or structures of the collective unconscious, of which Jung said,

> this part of the unconscious is not individual but universal; in contrast to the personal psyche it has contents and modes of behaviour that are more or less the same everywhere and in all individuals. It is . . . identical in all men and thus constitutes a common psychic substrate of a suprapersonal nature which is present in every one of us. (CW, 9, para. 3)[29]

The astrologer's hypothesis is that the planets and signs represent these modes of behavior or psychic and behavioral forms that are shared by all humans. Thus, we can use astrological knowledge to refine our patterns of behavior. An archetype is what I would call an innate predisposition. According to Stevens:

> Jung asserted that all the essential psychic characteristics that distinguish us as human beings are with us from birth. These typically human attributes Jung called archetypes. . . . [Individuation means] to develop what is already there, to actualize the archetypal potential already present in the psycho-physical organism, to activate what is latent or dormant in the very substance of the personality, to develop what is encoded in the genetic make-up of the individual, in a manner similar to that by which a photographer, through the addition of chemicals and the use of skill, brings out the image impregnated in a photographic plate.[30]

Astrologers are like the photographer developing film, using skillful interpretation to draw out the meanings and images that are implicitly

present in the natal pattern, identifying specific archetypes and potentials waiting to become manifest and visible. Stevens also asserts that:

> [A]rchetypes [are] the neuropsychic centres responsible for
> co-ordinating the behavioural and psychic repertoires of our
> species in response to whatever the environmental circum-
> stances we may encounter. . . . As Jung himself insisted, the
> term archetype 'is not meant to denote an inherited idea, but
> rather an inherited mode of functioning, corresponding to the
> inborn way in which the chick emerges from the egg, the bird
> builds its nest, a certain kind of wasp stings the motor ganglion
> of the caterpillar, and eels find their way to the Bermudas. In
> other words, it is a pattern of behaviour' (CW 18, para. 1228).[31]

Astrology aids us in embodying and expressing these essential modes
of functioning. Planets and zodiacal signs and describe what Stevens
terms behavioral forms or modes of behavior; they symbolize various
behavioral and psychic repertoires. Stevens continues:

> [A]rchetypes are meaning-creating imperatives. . . . [A]rche-
> types . . . are common to all humankind, yet we all experience
> them in our own particular way. . . . Jung stressed that the
> archetype was not an arid, intellectual concept but a living,
> empirical entity, charged not only with meaningfulness but
> also with *feeling*. . . . The archetypal endowment with which
> each of us is born presupposes the natural life-cycle of our
> species—being mothered, exploring the environment, playing
> in the peer group, adolescence, being initiated, establishing a
> place in the social hierarchy, courting, marrying, childrearing,
> hunting, gathering, fighting, participating in religious rituals,
> assuming the social responsibilities of advanced maturity, and
> preparation for death. 'Ultimately,' Jung wrote, 'every individ-
> ual life is at the same time the eternal life of the species' (CW
> 11, par. 146). . . . Jung . . . concluded that [archetypes] must cor-

respond to 'typical dispositions', 'dominants' or 'nodal points' within the structure of the psyche itself.[32]

Astrology illuminates this eternal life of the species as each person uniquely experiences it. Stevens suggests that these archetypal forms and patterns are emotionally charged and possess generative force. I've found that astrological symbols, especially when linked with dream images, have potency and create a force field for change. Studying planetary placements and cycles allows us to discern the timing of specific archetypes manifesting, for the purpose of conscious evolution.

Astrologers see parallels between planetary influence and archetypal forms. Following the movements of the planets lets us witness archetypal process at work and participate in it, so we can consciously develop within these typical dispositions. People who are stuck in inertia, depression, addictions, fixations, and other psychological maladies can gain an evolutionary stimulus through alignment with these change principles. That's what I'll illustrate in this chapter through several examples.

The archetypal structure and personal organization symbolized by the birth pattern take form as an individual's work, occupation, or vocational path. The archetype also manifests in dreams, in our unconscious life, as a force that seeks to shape our state of consciousness. For astrologers, the planetary and zodiacal archetypes are formative templates. To study the natal chart and transits is to allow one's body, mind, and intentions to take the shape of the various archetypes. Astrology is the most precise map of each individual's archetypal configurations for growth, and the only system that accurately describes the element of timing.

Before getting into the details of how I combine astrology and dreams as a therapeutic methodology, let me briefly note two archetypes especially pertinent to the study of astrology that emerge from the work of Dane Rudhyar: the archetype of time and the archetype of the birth chart itself. Rudhyar's work on cycles showed that there's a structure and organization to the flow of time. The cycle as a whole, exemplified by the lunation cycle, constitutes the template or archetype of time, with its identifiable rhythms and phases—especially the New

Moon, the moment of inception; the waxing phases of effort, overcoming inertia and resistance, and building structures; the Full Moon is the time of culminations and the cycle's peak intensity, followed by the waning, deconstructing, reorienting stages, and the cycle's conclusion in a state of release, letting go, and anticipation of the future. Time is the central archetype of our field—the pattern of change that provides the foundation for our entire enterprise.

Rudhyar also showed that the unfolding of personality has a structure and organization defined by the horoscope, which itself forms an archetype. He wrote:

> The symbolic meaning of the birth chart of an individual . . . is actually, and as far as its psychological value is concerned, an archetype in his unconscious. It is perhaps the most powerful of all archetypes, when it is brought up to the light of consciousness, inasmuch as it can determine the entire conduct of the individual, his entire attitude toward himself and his life, and the quality of his expectancy with reference to future events and his destiny as a whole.[33]

Studying the patterns of the birth moment and its progressed derivatives, we can conduct ourselves in a manner most conducive to actualizing this guiding template for development. Later, in Chapter 5, we'll examine how the complex personality archetype and spiritual potentials shown in the birth chart takes form in a career or occupational path. Here we're concerned with how dream characters and themes reflect planetary symbolism and emerge synchronistically at times of astrological significance. Astrology contributes to depth psychology the momentous insight that we can anticipate the emergence of specific archetypes and thus consciously participate in these evolutionary patterns and scripts.

Lunar Dreams

Awareness of planetary movements and cycles makes it possible to predict when a certain archetype is manifesting. Let's consider the central, primordial archetype experienced by all humans, which is

Mother, astrologically linked to Moon. Everyone comes from mother, and has the experience of womb gestation, birth, holding attachment, feeding, and the fulfillment or the frustration of our basic needs. The lunar archetype represents our instinctual seeking of a tender maternal embrace. It manifests as our memory of either receiving love and gratification by mother, or of being deprived of maternal affection and receiving cold, harsh, or ambivalent treatment. Typically our inner mother *imago* contains a mix of both sides, the good mother and the terrible mother. The memory and the experience of mother, and the feelings associated with her, is embedded in each person's unconscious and is portrayed in dreams—especially during transits to natal Moon, when the archetype is activated in dream images portraying women, a mother, one's own mother, a mother-child dyad, or in images evoking our experience of secure or insecure emotional attachment.

For example, while transiting Saturn opposed her natal Moon in Cancer, Gwen dreamed, "*I saw my mother and she had a very large mouth, gaping open.*" Gwen commented that her mother is a very needy person, especially now that she is elderly, and makes many demands on Gwen's time. The open mouth is reminiscent of the oral stage of infancy with its hungry, sucking, engulfing quality. Gwen has two children, now young adults, who still need her financial support, plus she says she has a needy husband. She is the need-fulfilling source for all the hungry, open mouths that need to be fed. And of course she has needs too. Reflecting on the dream, she felt care and concern for all of them, including herself. This example illustrates the deepening of meaning that characterizes humanistic astrology and a depth psychological approach. Instead of viewing transiting Saturn opposite the Moon as a "bad" transit, we view it as an opportunity to clarify and enhance her emotional experience and her feelings about family attachments. When Moon is involved, the story of the moment is generally about souls seeking comfort in one another and learning to find comfort in oneself.

Danielle had natal Moon conjunct Uranus and Saturn, and was approaching her first Saturn return. She was currently experiencing transiting Saturn conjunct her Moon. Danielle dreamed:

I'm at my grandmother's retirement community and see my aunt—who in real life has four kids, all with different fathers, and neglects them. In the dream I'm watching younger siblings and cousins, like I'm babysitting them. My aunt has a new child I didn't know about and she leaves the baby outside. The baby falls in a bathtub with arms stuck behind him. I pick him up by his hands. I have to be careful how I hold this fragile infant. I play babbling with him. I'm infuriated with my aunt and tell her off for leaving the baby here unattended and unannounced.

Danielle
Natal Chart
September 28, 1987
Tropical   Porphyry   Mean Node

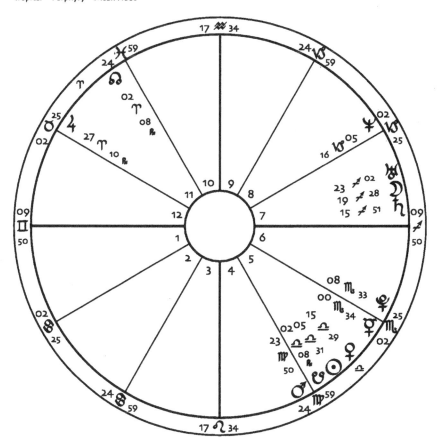

Danielle said, "My aunt has gone off the deep end into drugs. Two of her kids are in foster care. She's unprepared for motherhood. It reminds me of how my fiancé is ready to have kids but I'm not ready. I want to be prepared and in the right space to do it, not like my aunt, or my mother. Mom was my best friend, but when I was 19 she left all of us kids, abandoned us; she left us in a hotel and drove off. We were left to our own devices. This is on my mind lately because I'm turning thirty. I was raised to be a caregiver. [Think of Danielle's Moon conjunct Saturn.] The dream about my Aunt and my mother reminds me of irresponsible mothers pawning off responsibilities, and that relates to my own fear of having kids." The dream portrays Danielle's expression of warmth and tenderness in how she cares for the baby, carefully holding him, showing emergence of her own mothering, nurturing capacity. The dream shows a need to address developmental stresses stemming from feeling abandoned by her mother, and her perception of the difficulties faced by mothers. The dream highlights that her development at this time is proceeding in in accordance with the archetype of mother and motherhood—either acceptance or refusal of this role, with all of the emotional transformations this process entails. During the transit of Saturn conjunct Moon her evolution and individuation was shaped by emergence of this central archetype. That this process was somewhat emotionally complex and difficult stems from her natal Moon conjunct Saturn and Uranus, showing the tension between maternal obligations and a longing for emotional freedom. Saturnian themes are also evident in the dream: decisions and responsibility. But a lifetime of reflection on the lessons of Saturn has taught me that it's possible to love what we're responsible for, because it helps define our life's purpose.

Saturnine Dream Images

Saturn is a key planetary archetype that influences our development at every stage of life, signifying work, structure, responsibility, social adaptation and conformity, and practical manifestation. While transiting Saturn was conjunct her midheaven, a young woman named Jasmine dreamed:

I'm at my old office in San Francisco. My former boss Tracy is going to rehire me, but then she decides she isn't going to. I'm surprised and upset. I walk up this tall stairway and see her behind a professional-looking oak desk. She has great authority.

Tracy is a successful salesperson in Jasmine's industry, a role model, a career woman, signifying Jasmine's quest for advancement as an aspiring professional (climbing the tall staircase). Sitting behind this big oak desk signifies Tracy's authority as a woman who has made it. The oak desk symbolizes Jasmine's ambitions and career strivings, her efforts to advance within social organizations and hierarchies, very appropriate to the transit of Saturn to her Midheaven. The oak desk signified power, success, occupational fulfillment, and being solidly rooted.

During his Saturn return, a time of maturation, a young man named Dan was struggling financially and was somewhat ambivalent and uncommitted in a 4-year relationship. Dan dreamed *"A group of men in suits are sitting around a round table, talking about 'city planners.'"* Saturn (and its sign Capricorn) represents organizing, managing, achieving. It's our inner executive function, which manages projects and pursues specific ambitions and achievements. Saturn's influence brings a serious attitude toward life, a sense of industry, focus, patience, endurance, and persistence. Within two years Dan got a promotion and a nice raise at work, married his girlfriend, and purchased a house. He became effective in life planning.

Neptune in Dream Images

In contrast to the concerns of Saturn, Neptune and its zodiacal sign of Pisces represent the wholeness in which there's no differentiation, a state of nonduality. It also represents states of liquidity, uncertainty, confusion, indecisiveness, or spaciness. During Neptune transits and progressions, we may have healing dreams, and often we experience an intensification of dream images, especially water images—baths, showers, sprinkling, swimming, immersion in water, baptism. The Jungian interpretation, expressed by esteemed authors such as Edward Edinger and Gareth Hill, is that water dream images symbolize the presence and influence of the unconscious and the potential for restoration of our original wholeness. Neptune is the planet of dreams and its influence is often felt at times of dreams with evocative spiritual themes and imagery—which may include archetypal figures such as the seer, mystic, suffering savior, or martyr. When this archetype is active it may be a time to suffer our suffering consciously, with great tenderness and compassion.

The Dream of Water in a Room without Walls

The next example explores a story originally discussed in my book *Dreamwork in Holistic Psychotherapy of Depression*, and features work with the archetypal energies of several planets simultaneously. Vida was experiencing grief, depressed mood, and low self-esteem while going through a divorce and adjusting to life as a single mother. While transiting Neptune was conjunct her Moon in Pisces in the 7th house, and Pluto was square her Libra Sun, Vida dreamed:

> *I'm in a room of baths, wading in waist-deep water, swaying in a room without walls. There are brightly lit pillars, ornately tiled. Two women are entering with me into this hidden place we're exploring. I'm new to this space. It's a woman's space with candles, incense, flowers. Another woman is beautiful, with wavy, thick, silky black hair, a black skirt, dark skin, and dark eyes, secure and penetrating. She approaches and says, "Do you want oil in your hair?" I wonder, "Is this okay? Is anyone approaching?" I'm drawn toward her. It feels weird. She says, "Look, I have oil in my hair." I think to myself that might be okay.*

Vida's dream took place in a healing environment, a place of feminine mysteries. The tiled walls, flowers, candles, and incense form an inviting and sacred atmosphere and suggested to Vida the value of creating an aesthetically pleasing atmosphere and creating some form of personal healing ritual. In keeping with transiting Neptune conjunct her Moon, the dream portrayed what Gareth Hill has called a *watery ini-*

tiation, representing an emotional return to the mother, to a place of self-acceptance and emotional reconciliation with oneself; it indicates a moment of self-forgiveness. Dreams of water evoke the experience of spiritual renewal through "watery initiations, 'night sea journeys,' or 'dark nights of the soul' that move a person toward an inner orientation and . . . a state of renewed union with one's own wholeness."[34]

Vida's dream depicted *a room without walls*, a boundaryless space that reflects the influence of transiting Neptune. I felt that the dream wanted to tell her that there were no limits or barriers to her possibilities for growth. In the dream she met a dark woman representing her individuated identity. The woman's strong, penetrating eyes signified becoming inwardly secure in who she is, reflecting Pluto's transit to her natal Sun. In this dream's healing space Vida was swaying, an image suggesting ecstasy or euphoria, the expansive mood of Moon-Neptune—presenting a vivid contrast to her recent depressed, contracted emotional state. The dark woman in the dream emanated power, strength, beauty, and self-confidence, and she invited Vida to be initiated through anointment of her hair with oil. Anointment is a religious act of sanctifying the physical body. There was something so healing about treating her own body as holy and sacralized. Vida felt an urge to connect with this beautiful, strong woman but she was apprehensive about whether anyone was watching, and if it was okay to put oil in her hair. When I asked why she thought maybe it wouldn't be okay, Vida said she feared that if she stepped into the strength, beauty, elegance, and power this dream character embodied it would be off-putting to other women, who might feel threatened by her.

She said, "That reminds me of my mother. I always have to tone myself down so I don't overshadow her. She hated being a mother and let us know it, all the time. But nowadays Mom is into oils and scents, just like the woman in the dream." The dream during Neptune's transit to natal Moon evoked the image and the emotional atmosphere of Vida's mother, her charged complex of feelings around mother, and her experience of diminishing herself to ease mother's anxiety—which was exactly the same thing she'd done in her marriage. The dream portrays her perception of her mother's essence and potential, which was currently obscured by mother's resentment and negativity. This strong, determined woman also represented Vida's own potential. I told her, "I think the dream is saying it's okay for you to enter this healing space with your mother and with other women, to anoint yourself, and to allow yourself to become a goddess."

At this time in her life, Vida was preoccupied with financial pressures, isolation, and blaming herself for her husband's uncontrolled, untreated alcoholism. Her dream conveyed an alternative view of her situation from the perspective of the deep unconscious and a vision of her true essence, which was self-reliant and inwardly centered. This dream's Neptunian images of women bathing and anointing their hair was revitalizing, and it was no surprise to me that Vida soon established a new relationship and was married again within two years. It's also worth noting that during the transit of Pluto square natal Sun in Libra she discovered the inner strength and courage to deconstruct her old life, end one marriage, and begin another. Contemplating the dream coinciding with these pivotal transits was a turning point in her emotional and relational evolution.

Mars and Dream Symbolism

During transits or progressions involving Mars it's typical to encounter aggressive, contentious people and situations both in waking life and in dreams. Mars signifies exercise of the will as an individual, self-assertion, initiative, and motivation, and when Mars is a dominant planetary influence, one may dream of a soldier, warrior, or athlete, a competitor or adversary, a person with an angry demeanor, dream images of aggression, enmity, and discord; or we have dreams featuring sexual drives and experiences. We encounter the warrior and we become the warrior, asserting and standing up for ourselves.

For example, while transiting Uranus in the 7th house squared his natal Mars in Scorpio in the 4th house, Doug was angry at his longtime girlfriend, Lucy, but said nothing to her about it. Their relationship had been nonsexual for a number of years and Lucy had started going on dates with other men, but Bruce kept quiet. He'd suffered some extreme physical abuse as a child and had always suppressed anger, considering its expression dangerous and unacceptable. He feared becoming a ber-serk rageaholic like his father. While transiting Uranus squared natal Mars, he dreamed, "*There was a cloudy, grey window, behind which I saw a man with a red face.*" The red face reminded him of unexpressed hurt feelings and jealous anger, which seemed fully appropriate in his situation. The dream suggested there was within him some smoldering Mars fire. When he told Lucy directly that he didn't want her seeing other men, she said, "Until now you've given me no indication whatso-ever that you care about our relationship." Discussion of the symbol of the red-faced man prompted the insight that Doug needed to generate and express a more active sexual drive in order to maintain Lucy's inter-est. More broadly, under the incitement of Uranus square natal Mars, Bruce came to realize the importance of achieving a higher degree of vitality and physical fitness. Coming to terms with this dream image during the Uranus-Mars transit had beneficial results.

Astrology and Dreams in Couples Therapy

The next example illustrates how working with astrology and dreams together in couples therapy can be a potent practice that gives partners a window into each other's feelings and perceptions. Ed and Janet were seriously considering a divorce. They argued frequently, and both were dissatisfied with their marriage. Ed felt tremendous pressure financially and was constantly worried about the future. Janet felt neglected by Ed, who seemed to prefer the company of his guitar; she complained of a lack of closeness and physical intimacy. While transiting Saturn was in her 7th house conjunct natal Mars in Scorpio, Janet dreamed:

> *Ed and another man are sitting on the floor playing a game, involving moving around a game piece—a scorpion. Ed loses the game. The scorpion now gets to bite or sting you. The scorpion stung him, so there was immediate risk for losing the game. There could be long-term, chronic danger.*

The dream depicts playing a game of chance or risk, which appeared to be a comment from the unconscious on their relationship and the risks they were playing with. Janet's response was that the scorpion reminded her of her own anger.

The scorpion symbolized poisonous resentments and the danger these posed to their marriage. Janet resented that people liked Ed and held him in high esteem despite his ignoring his wife while she did all the shopping, cooking, and household chores, rarely volunteering to help out. She held a lot of resentment about that. But everyone thought Ed was such a great guy. She said, "If they only knew." Working with this dream along with the symbolism of transiting Saturn conjunct Mars deepened the couples therapy because the symbolism of the scorpion and Mars in Scorpio allowed us to openly discuss Janet's anger and the origins of specific grievances. In the dream, Ed lost the game, which brought the insight that he'd have much to lose if this marriage ended. Knowing the timing of the transit was helpful because they could trust that the contentious, inflamed feeling between them was emerging during a phase of heightened stress on their relationship that would hopefully ease up once the heated Mars transit concluded. Many couples break up at this point, not realizing that the time of conflict may be just a phase. Ed and Janet stayed together and said they felt more closely bonded than ever.

Sun: The King, The Queen, and the Golden Child

Archetypally, Sun signifies the golden child that grows into a King or Queen. When adequately supported and validated by the reflected light of the Moon, each person can grow into a Sun King or Sun Queen, endowed with positive self-esteem, a feeling of innate dignity. To know and live one's natal Sun is to be happy to be yourself, capable of self-expression and creative emanation. Activation of the natal Sun represents identity achievement, forming our defined attributes, talents, interests and objectives. Sun represents the experience or process of self-validation and self-expression, and positive extraversion—exteriorizing oneself so that others can see you and recognize you.

Douglas, a shy college student suffering from depression and low self-esteem, was experiencing transiting Jupiter squaring his natal Sun-Pluto opposition. He dreamed:

> *I was in a royal court with an elegant carpet where a king would sit, and I was dressed in a suit of armor, with a shield but no weapon. I am doing battle with the Japanese god Susena, fending off attacks.*

The royal court reminded Doug of success, becoming an authority figure, and also his father, who was ruler of the household, the person everyone relied on. The king represented power and his hope of becoming a central personality in family, friendship, and the workplace—someone important in the world and to others. In Japanese mythology, Susena is a god of storms, and here represents Doug's ongoing stormy emotional upheavals and lifelong anxiety issues. Encountering Susena's attacks reminded him of his father's anger and disappointment, his fierce temper, and Doug's own tendency to become angry at himself. The dream portrays how attacks on his sense of self-worth come from the inside, corresponding to the natal symbolism of Sun opposite Pluto. The image of wearing armor evoked the warrior archetype. Doug said that this armor represented his way of being guarded and closed off to people, but he also felt that it symbolized toughness, resilience, valor, and the courage to be himself. Transits to the Sun can bring about changes in our capacity for self-validation—affirmation of specific traits, interests, and commitments that define our identity. For Doug, one important moment in this process was that he overcame his fear of speaking in front of a group and gave a lucid, impassioned presentation in one of his college classes, receiving some positive feedback and acknowledgment, and lighting the spark of confidence that comes from "knowing who I am."

Roger, age 58, had been employed for decades as a shopkeeper, taking over the family business from his father, and was now contemplating a career change and pursuing graduate school in psychology. Roger had Sun conjunct Jupiter, Saturn, and Mercury in Capricorn, and at the time we met, Saturn and Pluto in Capricorn were transiting these natal planets. Roger told me this dream:

> *I'm in a dark, cold, dreary place, almost like a scene from a Dickens novel, and I was approached by two beggar women. They transformed, one into a king, a ruler of a far away country. I asked him why he had come to me. He said that he needed my help in saving him, and his kingdom. He said he was slowly being poisoned by someone in his kingdom. I was there with several people, one of whom resembled my brother, Daniel. I approached a pair of tall double doors adorned with a cross. I went inside and saw there were three cloistered priests who were not very friendly, not very holy. I sensed they were being very protective of a secret power. It was also clear they were representatives of a larger body—the Church. In the middle of the room was what appeared to be a shipwreck with a cabin door also adorned with a cross. The wreck was ancient. The wood was distressed and in an advanced state of decay. The priests weren't welcoming and were very guarded. My brother Daniel dashed past them, jumped onto the ship's deck, opened the cabin door and disappeared for a moment. When he returned he was bearing what I can only describe as the Holy Grail. The priests were up in arms, but could do nothing, as they knew we were under the protection of the king. They were guarding this relic of power, but couldn't find it, or simply couldn't open the cabin door. It was then discovered that they (the priests) were the ones poisoning the king. Having uncovered the plot, the priests were swiftly dealt with. I don't recall if they were banished or executed.*

Many aspects of this dream's symbolism match and correspond to Roger's natal Sun conjunct Saturn and Jupiter and the current transit of Saturn and Pluto conjunct natal Sun-Jupiter. The beggar women reflected impoverished self-esteem and the need to build a stronger sense of solar identity, to transform into a king and thus to "save the kingdom." The king is an image of the Self and Roger's potentials to establish a more

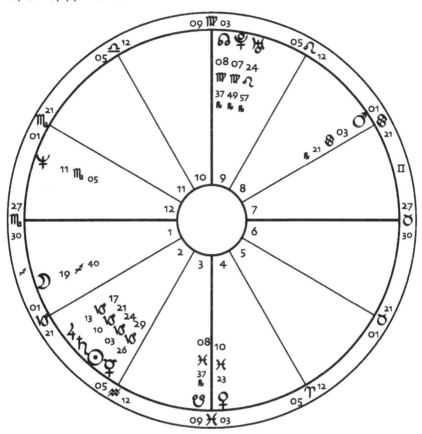

Roger
Natal Chart
January 14, 1961
Tropical   Porphyry   Mean Node

defined identity and to have dominion over his own life, including the choice to pursue a new professional role in a field other than his father's occupation. The king reminded Roger of his father, who had always lorded it over him and judged him. Saving the kingdom meant recovering a sense of dignity and self-respect, which was being poisoned by the demons of self-judgment and self-criticism. Poison suggests toxic emotions. The double doors adorned with a cross reminded him of his strict religious upbringing, early religious education, disillusionment with the church, but also his own quest for holiness. The unfriendly cloistered priests reminded him of Jesuit priests who had been his schoolteachers and persecutors, but it also reminded Roger of his isolation and high degree of reserve in social interactions. He hadn't been in a relationship in a number of years and was cloistered in that sense. Pluto (the hermit of the underworld) is at his Midheaven, and forms a close sesquiquadrate aspect to natal Saturn, symbolizing his experience of a strict, exacting, judgmental father and the unfriendly priests who oppressed and exercised their power over him in childhood, darkening his sense of sunny optimism (Sun-Jupiter), causing him to form a very serious, austere demeanor. The dream conveyed the insight that it was the priests that were poisoning the king.

The ancient shipwreck adorned with a cross has distressed wood, representing the ways Roger felt that his life had, in many ways, been a shipwreck, and that many youthful drives and dreams had gone unfulfilled. The shipwreck was a symbol of his recurrent states of depression. I've detailed in my other writings how dreams heal us through their portrayal of our suffering and woundedness and allow us to see and feel more clearly how we're hurting.[35] Inwardly acknowledging the significance of this image of the wounded self brought Roger some emotional relief. I reminded him that for decades he'd worked long hours and ably managed the family business, fulfilling the requirements of hard, focused labor demanded by his natal aspect of Saturn and Pluto. I wanted him to appreciate his own strength and dedication, and allowing this message to soak in, Roger experienced a moment of self-validation, a positive outcome during any transit to the natal Sun.

The culmination of the dream occurs when his brother returns bearing the Holy Grail, a symbol of wholeness that aptly portrays Roger's potential to reinvent and transform identity during the transits of Saturn and Pluto to his natal Sun. Now that the poisonous influences of childhood religious indoctrination and a lifetime of internal judgments were being exposed, he was free to make choices that would enable him to form a new life path and possibly a new occupation as an outgrowth of his new interests in depth psychology.

On the morning of her 21st birthday, with transiting Jupiter conjunct her natal Sun-Venus conjunction, a woman dreamed, *I was in a church wedding wearing a beautiful white wedding dress with a large gold crown.* This amazing image was a vision of her solar essence and potentials, her spiritual wholeness, and her aspirations to marriage, and featured the emergence of the royal archetype in the image of the gold crown—representing individuation and alchemical transformation of the self.

Under transits or progressions involving the Sun, dreams often feature a celebrity, royalty, or star personality. Many years ago, when transiting Jupiter opposed my natal Sun and conjoined natal Uranus, I dreamed that *"The actor Jack Nicholson comes over to me, reaches out to shake my hand, gives me a fantastic smile, and says, "How ya' doin'?!"* This image showed me a path toward wholeness, beyond a state of shy introversion and relatively bland, colorless behavior, and signaled that it was okay for me to become a more outgoing, Uranian personality. Jack Nicholson has natal Sun closely conjunct Uranus and he's a true original. He is like no other. He has realized his own archetype. Obviously, I'm nothing like Jack, but his appearance in my dream symbolized a potential of the Sun—to shine, to emanate, to become a star, a light source, a more fully realized and distinctive individual.

Uranus and Dream Imagery

As described by Dane Rudhyar, in his book *The Sun is Also a Star,* Uranus is a symbol of individualized life and transpersonalized life, and represents availability to whatever has to happen. Uranus overcomes Saturnian limits to solar energy, to the radiating power of the Sun. Uranus releases energy, inspires us, and keeps our path to the galactic center open. It represents discontinuity with the past, a new orientation, and often a visitation of the spirit. Uranus is a power of transfiguration that releases light through the personality.[36]

Rudhyar often noted that an individualizing person's path is sometimes discordant with social norms. Under the influence of Uranus, we choose more exciting but less stable paths, and become unconventional, progressive. Sometimes a Uranian person experiences the wound of being different or controversial.

Jack Nicholson
Natal Chart
April 22, 1937
11:00:00 AM EST
Neptune, New Jersey
40N13 / 74W02
Tropical   Koch   Mean Node

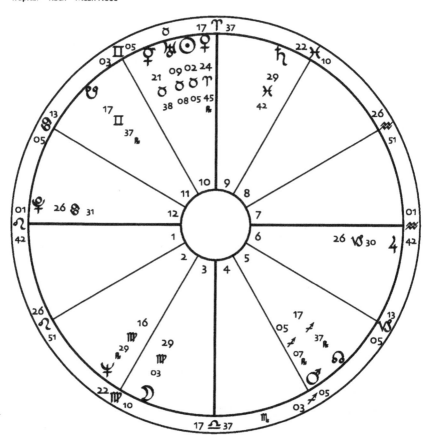

While transiting Uranus crossed his MC, a visual artist named Ken dreamed:

I'm at my workplace. In the back there's a metal shop. A guy is dressed in work clothes with welder's goggles. He's silver, covered with aluminum dust from head to toe. There's a big oven behind me, or a forge.

The silver man reminded Ken of the musician and actor Tom Waits in a silver costume on an album cover. Tom Waits was one of Ken's heroes and a personal symbol for liberated creativity—a man whose personality exudes sly humor, tenderness, alienation, and a sense of irony. The image of the oven or forge resonates to the Greek mythological figure of Hephaistos, the blacksmith, a wounded figure who walked with a limp and crafted armor for great heroes such as Achilles. Hephaistos represents the capacity to overcome adversity and suffering and to mold materials in fire, forging something enduring—in his case weapons of battle such as swords, shields, and armor. Ken and I concluded that as an artist he could express his authentic self and his innermost feelings, but he also needed the toughness to protect himself against the world's obstacles and naysayers and to stay connected to his own creative fire; he realized that he needed to spend some serious time in his studio, to stoke the fire to produce works of lasting value.

As an archetypal force, Uranus represents the trickster, rebel, revolutionary, inventor, and scientist. While transiting Uranus was conjunct her Sun, a young woman committed to becoming a visual artist despite her parents' disapproval of her occupational choice. She dreamed that *"a bird was eating my liver."* This dream symbolism directly parallels the myth of Prometheus, who stole fire from the gods and gifted it to humanity, and was punished by being chained to a rock where every day an eagle ate his liver. Richard Tarnas has linked Uranus to the Greek god Prometheus and this archetype clearly appears in her dream. Prometheus represented the agonies and ordeals of the creative process, and also her desire to spread fire and evoke a response in others through her paintings and digital artwork.

Pluto and Dream Symbolism

Pluto is the planetary symbol of death and rebirth, endings and renewal. He can appear as the criminal, dictator, or fascist, in images or acts of violence or brutality, or in dreams involving crisis and emergencies, or death. During the transit of Pluto opposite his natal Sun in Cancer in the 4th house (which natally was sesquiquadrate Pluto in Sagittarius), a young man named Scott dreamed:

I am in danger of turning into a zombie. There are zombies all around and if one of them touches you, you could turn into a zombie. A woman tells me the magic three words that will prevent this.

Scott told me that both his parents were heroin addicts and were like the walking dead; he viewed them as "complete degenerates." Both had turned to crime and served time in prison. Scott himself often felt numb, shut down, depressed, and isolated himself from others. When we discussed the dream, I told him that I thought perhaps the three magic words that would prevent him from becoming a zombie were "I love you"—words he longed to hear and longed to say to someone. Love is what would save him from a dark fate.

Pluto may manifest in dreams as the shadow, an encounter with evil, immorality, criminal elements, or scary dream characters, or dreams with themes of loss, bereavement, desolation, endings, and defeats of the ego.

The Dream of the Black Skull

In *Dreamwork and Self-Healing* I described a powerful dream image. When transiting Pluto was conjunct my natal Saturn, I learned that my father was gravely ill in the hospital, ten weeks before he passed away. I dreamed:

I'm with my wife, Diana, digging next to our house. I unearthed a black skull, with prominent jaw and teeth. It could have been the skull of a wolf or wolverine.

The skull of death was visibly present within my unconscious. This skull reminded me of a mask, like the collection of carved and painted masks that my father had in his study, and this made me aware that he would soon be entering the world of beloved ancestors. The skull's prominent teeth also reminded me of the night I went to see B.B. King perform at the Apollo Theatre in Harlem when I was thirteen years old.

I went with a longtime friend of B.B.'s and we had excellent seats up near the front, and I distinctly remember that while he played his guitar solos, B.B.'s face lit up in a beautiful smile with the colorful spotlights reflecting off his sparkling white teeth. After the show, we went backstage where the famous blues singer Big Mama Thornton was talking to herself and guzzling a bottle of whiskey. Frisky-looking women in tight dresses were fussing over their makeup. One of B.B.'s managers walked into the room and opened up a briefcase crammed with pornographic magazines, and made a big point of showing them to me. It was like I had entered a completely different, subterranean realm—a hip Afro-American underworld of music, sex, and booze. And when I was introduced to B.B., he shook my hand and let me play his guitar, Lucille. This actually happened. I'm not blowing steam here!

When I held Lucille backstage at the Apollo Theatre I had a cast on my right hand, because I'd recently fractured a finger in a basketball game. It was a Thursday evening in February 1971, and my mother rushed me to the Emergency Room at Roosevelt Hospital, where I saw people on stretchers with life-threatening injuries and illnesses, some being treated for gunshots and stab wounds. I shared a treatment room with a man bearing cuts and bruises from a barroom brawl, who talked to me as I sat waiting for the doctor to set my hand into a plaster cast. It was the night of a New Moon in Pisces, zodiacal sign of hospitals, disabilities, and feelings of sympathy and compassion for the suffering of others. And these memories and feelings were joined with awareness of my father lying at the edge between life and death in a hospital room. All of this was evoked by the dream symbolism of the black skull, while Pluto was conjunct my natal Saturn.

The Dream of the Bartender

The next example combines the archetypal meanings and symbolism of Neptune and Pluto. Rylee, age 25, consulted me in a state of shock and grief after her father died unexpectedly and tragically, and reported that she'd recently been snorting coke and binge-drinking with her friends. She was exhausted, hung over, and emotionally numb. At the time, transiting Pluto was passing several times over her natal Sun-Neptune conjunction in Capricorn and transiting Saturn was conjunct natal Venus and Mars. Pluto conjunct the Sun and Neptune brought initiation into awareness of death and a sense of being lost and confused in the absence of someone she loved dearly, describing her father as "my best friend." Pluto's conjunction with Neptune unleashed a desire to get wasted on drugs and alcohol, to numb her feelings, to create a temporary feeling of elation and stimulation to ward off sadness and depression. But this awakening of her Sun-Neptune also roused the

Rylee

Natal Chart
January 9, 1994
Tropical   Porphyry   Mean Node

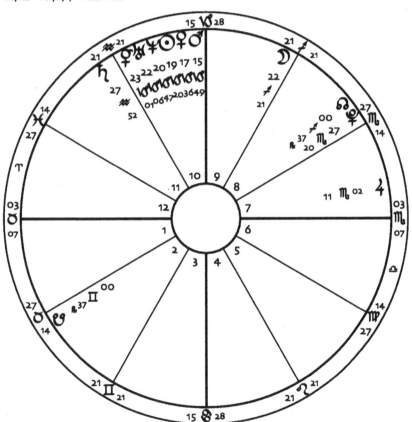

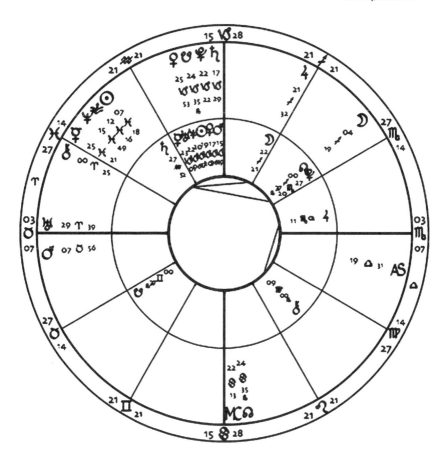

healing influence of the unconscious, which conveyed an important message through a simple but powerful dream: "*A bartender refused to serve me a drink and I became quite belligerent, throwing glasses at the barroom walls.*"

I said to Rylee, "Usually a bartender will refuse to serve a patron a drink for two reasons: either the person is too young, or the person has had enough to drink already. I think both are true for you. You're too young to be drowning your sorrows in a bar, and you've probably had enough already." She was already experiencing weakening health effects of her drug and alcohol binges and she was having trouble concentrating at work—more Neptune.

Over several months we grappled together with her efforts to maintain sobriety, I helped her locate local AA and grief support groups, and I suggested she reach out to her friends and support team and let them know "I'm going through a lot and I really need you in my life right now." This last strategy of asking for help proved to be most useful as she reestablished connections with several family members and began efforts to distance herself from friends who would tempt her into resuming bad habits. Under the fierce imperatives of Pluto's transit over her Sun and Neptune, Rylee endured this emotionally raw and existentially uncertain time with grace and gradual self-forgiveness. What also began to brighten up her horizons was that she noticed she was suddenly getting a lot of attention from men, under the planetary impetus of transiting Saturn conjunct her Venus-Mars. After several impulsive one-night stands, she felt the stirrings of desire for a more stable, mature relationship, and as transiting Saturn turned retrograde near Venus-Mars she began to see one man consistently, a man who didn't drink or do drugs.

Venusian Dream Images

During transits or progressions involving Venus we typically experience the archetype of love, encounter love goddess Aphrodite, and are stirred by beauty, art, music. Sometimes we see the Beloved in dreams, or images bringing appreciation of the rich beauty of nature. At these times, we seek peace, harmony and the creation and appreciation of graceful form in any medium. The Venusian archetype often appears in dreams of a beautiful, attractive person, a beloved spouse, lover, relative, or pet; or dreams about a relationship or a couple. It also signifies the Artist. Venus is the planetary symbol for the archetypal *anima*, embodied by a beautiful, captivating figure of either gender who stirs *eros*, a heightened feeling of attraction, fascination, longing, and a desire for union. With her Sun conjunct Venus and Mars, Rylee (discussed above) was someone who embodied the anima and tended to stir a lot of attraction from others. Murray Stein wrote: "If the image of the shadow instills fear and dread, the image of the anima/us usually brings excitement and stimulates desire for union. It engenders attraction.... We want to be part of it, we want to join it." [37] Anima manifests in dream characters we're very attracted to, who inspire us and ignite our passions. This person (or dream figure) moves us, and stirs our feelings and romantic longings. But where many people look for a spouse or lover to carry the enlivening anima, it's also possible to unfold this archetype by finding what *animates* us and brings us alive—a source of pleasurable fulfillment. In my own life, I live the anima through music, guitar, composing songs, playing in jazz bands, as well as through marriage. Venus is a central archetype in my chart, as it trines my Ascendant and aspects my Sun, Moon, and several other planets.

The Dream of the Lace Curtain, an Open Book, and the Refined Woman's Painting

This example is also adapted from *Dreamwork and Self-Healing*. Years ago, when transiting Saturn squared natal Venus I had this dream:

> *I climbed a staircase to a room in a tower or turret. I walked into a room where a very refined, beautiful woman with long hair had left an open book and one of her watercolor paintings sitting on a table. She wasn't in the room, but I was hoping to see her.*

This dream reminded me of several artistic women I'd loved in the past and my feeling of emotional resonance with them. The refined woman and the watercolor painting suggested purity, sensitivity, and artistic inspiration—qualities suggesting the presence of anima. The refined woman reminded me of Saraswati, Indian goddess of art, music, philosophy, culture, and education—all pursuits that inspire me. The open book represented my desire to be more emotionally open with other people, to let others see me, and to make myself accessible in my writing, teaching, and everyday demeanor. At the same time, climbing the stairs to the room in the tower reminded me of my habit of entering a private, solitary space to read, write, meditate, and study music. The dream brought me in touch with my inner anima, the part of myself that's artistic and creative.

Anima is the urge in us to create beauty—beauty that pierces the soul. It represents our human capacity to make life more meaningful, more expansive, more exalted, by creating graceful artistic forms. Art and music ennoble our existence, and make us feel everything more vividly and intensely. The archetypal Venusian energy that sometimes emerges from the unconscious in dreams can also manifest as harmonious creative expression in life, a topic to which we'll return in Chapter 6.

Astrology, Synchronicity, and Dreams

Astrology and dreams both are governed by the principle of *synchronicity*, a meaningful coincidence of events, where a complex of seemingly unrelated occurrences cluster together at a certain time moment, connected by the presence of an archetypal theme or energy that charges that moment with meaningfulness.[38] Astrologers observe the complex of events coinciding with celestial phenomena such as a Full Moon, Mercury retrograde, a Saturn return, or Mars-Pluto aspect. All astrological techniques assess the forces coalescing in a given moment, and how they visibly manifest in experiences resonant with the archetypal symbolism of the planets. For example, once, at the exact time of a Full Moon in Aries, conjunct Uranus in Aries, I was returning home after a walk with my dog Kona, and while searching my pockets for the keys to the front door I fumbled the leash for a split second, and Kona suddenly darted at blazing speed across the street and bit another dog that was passing by with its owner, drawing blood. This attack was totally unprovoked, at least from my perspective. I assume that in Kona's canine mind she was protecting her pack and its turf from a potential threat. In my mind it was an event fraught with potential financial and legal consequences. Regardless, it was an archetypal event of nature, embodying the principle that you must attack to survive. Aries represents the archetype of predator and prey—the will to live. Kona was enacting the archetype of pure Aries instinctual energy, which ignites us to act impulsively, without hesitation.

Marie-Louise von Franz noted that in synchronicities the unconscious breaks through into consciousness in creative ways that carry heightened psychic energy and psychological intensity.[39] In contemplating the links between dream symbols and planetary symbols we experience unconscious forces intensifying our lives and elevating our vital and psychic energy; and these manifestations of the unconscious are always shaped by archetypal situations, themes, and characters.

Here's another recent example: The night before leaving for a two-week vacation in Lake Tahoe, I dreamed that I saw a bear. On the final night of our vacation, while walking in a residential neighborhood I saw a bear across the street from me, ambling across somebody's lawn. We looked at each other for a moment, then the bear turned and headed into the woods, and I sprinted in the opposite direction. Thus, my dream image came true. It must be noted that bear sightings in Tahoe are not uncommon, so to some degree my own expectancy may have contributed to formation of this dream image. But an additional factor that made this close encounter a meaningful synchronistic event was that during my vacation I was studying mythology, preparing to teach a college course, and I'd recently spent hours watching videos of Joseph Campbell lectures, including talks in which he described the paleolithic cult of the cave bear, evidence of one of the earliest forms of prehistoric mythological thought. The encounter with the bear in Tahoe connected me to a mythical past, that time of human origins, which was now present time, sparking a feeling of awe and revitalization. Astrologically this emergence of the bear archetype corresponded to transiting Pluto in Capricorn conjunct my IC, which I interpret as a connection to archaic roots and ancient human origins, our historical past, and its present resonance. I returned to what Mircea Eliade calls *illo tempore*, the mythical time of origins. It was also relevant that I'd recently moved to a new house where I was enjoying deep sleep and felt newly connected to the domestic instincts of a hibernating bear.

In synchronicities and in dreaming, unconscious forces shock us to attention and fresh perceptions and a feeling of specific meanings that are conveyed by the intensity of the moment. The dream is what von Franz calls a "uniting fact," a focal point for a complex of inner and outer events occurring at a meaningful time moment that can be specified and understood astrologically.

Contemplating astrology and dreams together is a transformative practice that intensifies our emotions and taps creative energies. Now that we sense how archetypes linked to planetary symbols emerge within the unconscious as dream images, let us consider the manifestation of archetypes in daily life occurrences, as well as in the formation of work roles, careers, and defined vocational paths.

CHAPTER 4

Simplified Diurnal Astrology:
A Method for Practical Intelligence and
Efficiency in Daily Life

A strology is a practice where we transform one step after another
and then another, in an endless chain of learning situations.
In this chapter I discuss a simple technique that can guide our daily
actions and sharpen our responsiveness to evolutionary lessons in daily
life. Simplified Diurnal Astrology is an approach I developed decades
ago, at the very beginning of my studies. On any occasion when I have
the luxury of reflection, I stop, take a breath, and look at the chart of
the moment, observing, in a contemplative frame of mind, the rising,
culmination, setting, and anticulmination of transiting planets, which
pose a series of evolutionary lessons or "microscripts." I plan my next
move during the day or evening as I set my attention on specific tasks
and activities signified by angular planets as well as lunar aspects. This
practice has the capacity to make our use of time efficient and produc-
tive, leading to a multiplicity of satisfying outcomes. You accomplish
every task in its own time, deploying attention effectively in multiple
life domains. This is the astrology of the present time and how to maxi-
mize its potentials. Couples, friends, families, and groups of people can
follow the energy of the moment to harmonize and evolve together.

The main thing I look for in this method is transiting planets near
any of the four angles, cardinal points, or Moon's nodes; and the transiting Moon aspects to other transiting planets. This method is based
on the principle of angularity, an essential phenomenon in astrology
first elucidated by Cyril Fagan and Michel Gauquelin. Near the angles,
planets capture our attention. In a diurnal chart, planets placed within
10–15 degrees of the angles are accentuated. The key is not just to
observe the rising and setting and culmination of planets, but to move

with the changing sky, to resonate with the energy of whatever planets are foreground at that time.

What we're doing here isn't like traditional horary astrology in that there isn't a specific question, but more a broad question, what am I supposed to be doing right now? What is coming up? I don't follow traditional horary rules closely. I don't worry about whether the first three degrees of a sign or last three degrees are rising, or if the Moon is in the Via Combusta, although that might be relevant to other astrologers. I do note when the Moon is Void of Course (not forming any Ptolemaic aspects to other planets), as this often indicates an unfocused time when nothing of much consequence is likely to occur.

The diurnal technique is related to electional astrology because attunement to the daily motion and aspects of planets trains us to wait for an auspicious time for certain experiences, or to initiate certain actions. For example, when deciding to call to ask someone out on a date, it's better to refrain from calling when transiting Pluto is conjunct the diurnal Descendant—when you might experience the other person as cold, guarded, or rejecting. The best moment for a social connection is when Venus is on an angle, or better yet, during a Moon-Venus conjunction as it reaches a diurnal angle.

Applying electional principles, diurnal astrology can aid us in making well-timed actions. So, for example, if you want to talk to your boss about a raise, avoid holding a meeting during a Moon-Mars conjunction, square, or opposition, especially while these planets are rising, setting, or culminating. Or if you're planning an event and hope that people will show up, it's better not to schedule it during a waning, balsamic Moon or Void of Course Moon. If possible, the Moon should be increasing in light and, if it's a learning event such as a talk, class, or seminar, try to schedule it when Moon is aspecting Mercury or Jupiter. I often try to arrange social gatherings such as a party on days with a Moon-Venus conjunction, if I want this to be an occasion when people connect with each other.

The diurnal method I'm describing here is distinct from electional astrology insofar as it expands into an open-ended inquiry. Rather than electing a time for a specific event, I consider what event(s) the universe is electing to have happen now. I contemplate the sky and ask, "What does this moment call forth?" What does life want now? What is life presenting to me now? And what is my intention now? To answer these questions, I look at what planets are accentuated by angularity and lunar aspects, to sense where the energy is.

When Venus is on an angle, often a friend calls, or I reach out to someone. I have a pleasant interaction with my sweetheart. I play some music. I appreciate the beauty of my present circumstances or environment, something I try to do several times each day. Or I get cleaned up, put on fresh clothes, wash my hair, whatever will enhance my appearance. Similarly, when Moon aspects Venus, I feel serene, loving, affectionate, and I seek to satisfy emotional needs through friendship, beauty, art, and music. It's a time to express love and tenderness. Venus angular and aspects of Venus-Moon signify harmonious moments.

Contrast this to times when Mars is on an angle (or aspected by Moon), when there may be an energy or atmosphere of anger, stress, or discord. One evening I did a chart of the moment and a Moon-Mars conjunction in Sagittarius was setting, conjunct the Descendant, and my wife Diana suddenly got furious at me about some small infraction regarding how the laundry was sorted or put on the wrong temperature in the dryer, or not folded properly. I wasn't in the mood to get yelled at, so I took some reading matter and hurriedly left the house in my flip-flop sandals and parked my butt on the curb about a half a block away. At that exact instant, a bird sitting on a wire crapped on my shoulder. I looked up at him, and thought why is everybody against me right now? But knowing about Mars, I felt at peace. I tried to have a sense of humor as I went home and put on a clean shirt.

You'll learn a tremendous amount about the little clashes and irritations of life just by watching the rising, culmination, and setting of Mars, which flashes and flares up for a moment, and then the energy is discharged and the storm passes. Minor domestic flaps typically happen when Mars (or Pluto) is angular. There's a similar energy when transiting Moon aspects Mars. We tend to feel more energized, angry, impatient, and there can be a spark of sexual fire. People may be excitable, reactive, irritable, or angry if needs aren't being met.

When Mars is on an angle it's often a good time for some physical activity. This is when I feel like working out, exerting myself physically, working up a sweat. But if I try working out when Neptune is on an angle, I usually find that I'm fatigued, with no energy and drive or motivation to climb the hills. I just end up strolling, not accelerating and burning.

Diurnal astrology gets you outside the perspective of your own chart and into the flow of the present time, the background energy that everyone is feeling simultaneously. The diurnal chart describes what's happening in this place and time, so it sheds light on the astrology of collective events and things that happen in our community. For example, recently I went to a restaurant during a Moon-Mars conjunction in Gemini, and right as these planets culminated at the MC two cars collided in the parking lot outside REI and voices were raised; a few choice epithets were used. Everyone in the busy parking lot and a crowd seated outdoors at a nearby restaurant had their eyebrows raised while we witnessed this altercation. What I remember was the sickening sound of metal on metal. So under the angular ray of Mars there are clashes, crashes, mishaps, and dustups. You break a glass or stub your toe or cut yourself shaving or strain a muscle. That's life.

This method can reduce our fear of supposedly dreadful, malefic influences such as Mars, Saturn, and Pluto as we relate to these planetary energies and work with each of them effectively. For example, when Saturn is rising, culminating, setting, it's time for practical matters, getting chores done, organizing, getting things accomplished, straightening up. One day some years ago when Saturn was rising and the Moon was square Saturn, I remember I went to my mother's house and did errands, vacuumed her apartment, filed paperwork, watered the plants, and took out the garbage. Attunement to the daily rising, culmination, and setting of Saturn teaches us not to be afraid of Saturn energy but to use it constructively. We've all got a thousand and one little things that have to get done.

Similarly, during transiting Moon-Saturn aspects the energy of the moment would like to be focused and task-oriented. This is a time to stay grounded, stay on schedule, create order, attend to chores, and follow through to finish and accomplish things. Sometimes we feel sad, depressed, or aware of unsatisfied needs. Moon-Saturn calls forth a serious attitude and emotional strength; we have to take responsibility for our situation.

When Saturn is the archetypal dominant, the focus is on our life within form and structure. Trying to meditate when Saturn is angular isn't easy for me because that's a time when I really should be getting things done, straightening up. Similarly, trying to do a linear task such as balancing my checkbook or keeping other financial records while Neptune is angular is also a work against nature! I can't concentrate, make stupid calculation errors, get hopelessly lost and confused and befuddled when the numbers don't add up correctly at all, the accounts don't balance, or I end up falling asleep and face-plant onto my desktop calculator.

When Neptune is angular (or during Moon-Neptune aspects), I like to take a break. It's time to take a bath, meditate, take a nap, or veg out in front of the TV. I allow myself to do this, as long as I'm not driving, teaching class, or in a business meeting. But this is often a moment when one feels a need to sit or lie down and rest, or go to sleep. During Moon-Neptune aspects the mood is more fluid, liquid, spacious, suitable for contemplative activities such as reading fiction or studying astrology and mysticism. This is a moment to let go and inwardly surrender, to feel how we're part of everything. During Moon-Neptune aspects we may feel empathy, express altruism, and extend *metta*, loving-kindness, to others. Things are a little nebulous so we need to tolerate uncertainty in an open, receptive state. This is the perfect time for meditation.

In contrast to spiritual, expansive, or spacey and unfocused Neptunian phases, when Mercury is on an angle, or conjunct, square, or opposite the Moon, the tendency is to feel wired, busy, nervous, high strung, talkative, focused on thinking, writing, communication, documents, and traveling from place to place. It's time to be on the move, in transit. This is when I get tons of writing done, compose letters or emails, talk to someone, exchange some information. Also, I may need to get in the car and go someplace, get on the road. Trying to sleep when Mercury is setting or anti-culminating is counterintuitive as I usually just lie there awake thinking. This can be a great time to read in bed or write in a journal or have a bedtime conversation before going to sleep.

When Moon is angular in a diurnal chart it alerts me to attend to cooking, homecare, finding emotional and physical comfort and nourishment. For me, it signifies hanging out in the yard or the breakfast nook or on the front porch. It's a moment to enjoy our little habitats. I remember to call my mother, my aunt, or a supportive friend. I cook something and eat it. I pick up my clothes and do the dishes. I express feelings and needs. I create a secure base inside me and around me in my environment. This is the moment of care for home, care for the self, care for others. Moon signifies resting against our experience, settling into it, feeling it.

Tracking the transiting Moon's aspects fosters attunement to a deeply embodied *felt sense* of the present moment.[40] The Moon's natal aspects create in us a tendency to respond emotionally in conditioned patterns. Yet it's possible to experience a wide spectrum of emotional states that are synced to transiting Moon's conjunction, opposition, and square with the transiting planets. Awareness of our changing states and moods enables us to expand beyond our usual, conditioned emotional responses, so that we become more flexible and multifaceted. It's especially powerful to apply this same perspective to tracking the progressed Moon's phases and aspects to other planets, except the progressed Moon's aspects typically influence us for months, not just a day. The Moon's natal, transiting, and progressed aspects give astrologers a precise formula for developing emotional intelligence.

When Uranus is foreground in a diurnal chart, something unexpected occurs, there's a sudden reversal, something funny or incongruous happens; there's excitement and controversy, and you tend to chase whatever storm is brewing at that time. You want to do something your own way, breaking a pattern. You become aware of surprising, unexpected events in the social-political sphere. Transiting aspects of Moon and Uranus correspond with times of emotional excitability or when we feel an urge for freedom and independence. While Moon-Venus contacts show a need for closeness, Moon-Uranus aspects indicate a need for some distance or emotional separation. One seeks more emotional freedom, separation or differentiation from others.

Pluto foreground in a diurnal chart is one of the most interesting phenomena to observe. It's a moment for completions, getting rid of unwanted items, throwing out the garbage, disinfecting wounds, eradicating rodents and pests, stripping down, flushing out, bringing things out in the open to air out. Sometimes during Moon-Pluto aspects there's an experience of an emotional upset and resurfacing of buried feelings or memories; some feelings of bitterness, resentment, or negativity build up or need to be released. These are moments to detoxify and flush out blockages or impurities of body, speech, mind, and action. Pluto angular or Moon-Pluto aspects can stir emotional catharsis and intensification of feelings, and a need for emotional closure and completion. Sometimes we encounter power struggles, unpleasantness, or interpersonal issues of control or domination.

One afternoon, I cast the diurnal chart with Uranus exactly setting, square Pluto, which was exactly at the IC. As I considered what changes and unruly energies could be in store, I went and turned over our compost pile and took out the recycling and pruned rose bushes and did a bunch of weeding and clipping and cleanup, clearing, pruning to start over, to initiate new growth. Several months later, on the day of a Moon-Pluto conjunction, we sifted the compost and spread it on our fruit trees.

Another diurnal chart I cast featured Uranus conjunct MC, and Pluto setting. The combined influence of Uranus and Pluto often coincides with socio-political changes and upheavals. I turned on TV to hear news of Hurricane Sandy pummeling the east coast, leaving a swath of destruction; other news reports described bombings in Iraq, a broken truce in Syria, and possible skullduggery involving U. S. voting machines.

When Sun is foreground, I have consciousness of an objective, and strive to embody a specific zodiacal energy. Sun angular directs my attention to the evolutionary mission of whatever sign the Sun is passing through. Sun in Sagittarius: a learning objective, to be the educated one. Sun in Cancer: to be the nurturing, feeling, caring one. Sun in Aries: to be the strong-willed and determined one.

Simplified diurnal astrology teaches malleability, flexibility of attitude, and conscious, intentional shapeshifting through various archetypal situations. Where horary astrology answers specific questions, diurnal astrology considers the broader question: what am I supposed to be doing right now, and how can I activate all of my circuits in alignment with this present local sky? This approach transcends the individual chart and gets you outside the perspective of your natal patterns into the flow of the moment, the background energy that everyone is feeling at the same time. It can unify couples and families who learn to flow together in harmonious accordance with celestial order.

CHAPTER 5

Vocational Astrology and
Career Counseling Theory: A New Synthesis

With Saturn and Pluto now transiting in Capricorn it's an appropriate time to focus on vocational astrology—the art of guiding ourselves and our clients to fulfillment and success in the world of work, to aid career decision making, but also to cope with career setbacks and defeats, workplace stress, burnout, unemployment, changes of occupation, and retirement. After briefly reviewing some fundamentals, I'll discuss how career counseling theories can enhance vocational astrology, and how astrology expands career counseling, adding spiritual nuance and the crucial dimension of timing. Both fields support the idea that being satisfied with one's work or career is central to personal happiness.

I believe that whatever our vocational path, for success we need to awaken the powers of each planet. Mercury: good language and communication skills. Jupiter: expansion through education, planning, and expansive goal setting. Mars: energy, drive, initiative, motivation. Moon: caring and showing our concern for others, and staying in our emotional center. Venus: having good people skills, dressing well, tact and social appropriateness, mingling well with others and making a positive impression. And Saturn: focus, organization, and sustained effort. Neptune can be a force that's disruptive for some people or problematic for their career development, as it can manifest in behaviors and attitudes that undermine success, such as lethargy, defeatist attitudes, addictions, and disorganization. Neptune can endow us with spirituality, imagination, idealism, altruism, and a desire to be of service; but its unhealthy manifestations include oversensitivity, incompetence, idle fantasy, helplessness, alcohol and drug abuse, and vegetative TV and video game viewing.

In his classic text, *Vocational Guidance by Astrology*,[41] (first published in 1942, now reprinted in Noel Tyl's *Vocational Astrology for Success in the Workplace*.[42]), Charles Lunz writes that we should pay special attention to planets in the 10th house, planets near the Midheaven, planets in the 9th house but within 5° of the Midheaven; and planets aspecting the Midheaven. For example, Taylor Swift was born with Venus square her Midheaven. I broaden this by examining any planet in the foreground of the chart, within 5–10 degrees of any of the four angles, especially the Ascendant. For example, Microsoft founder Bill

Taylor Swift
Natal Chart
December 13, 1989
8:36:00 AM EST
Reading, Pennsylvania
40N20 / 75W56
Tropical   Porphyry   Mean Node

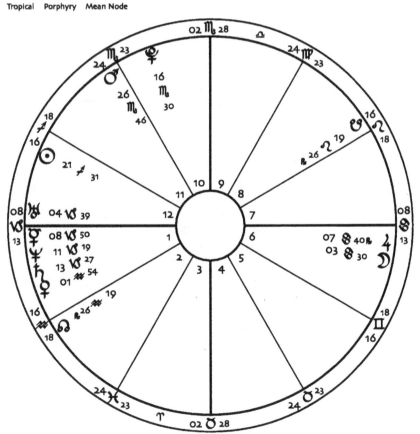

Gates has Uranus, planet of technology, innovation, computers, and media, conjunct his Ascendant.

Basketball superstar Stephen Curry has Mars square his Aries Midheaven.

Lunz says Saturn's sign and house placement should be considered and also planets in Capricorn, the sign associated with ambitions and career. I have natal Saturn in Sagittarius and my career arc has been as follows: proofreader in a publishing company, music teacher, astrology

Bill Gates
Natal Chart
October 28, 1955
10:00:00 PM PST
Seattle, Washington
47N36 / 122W20
Tropical Porphyry Mean Node

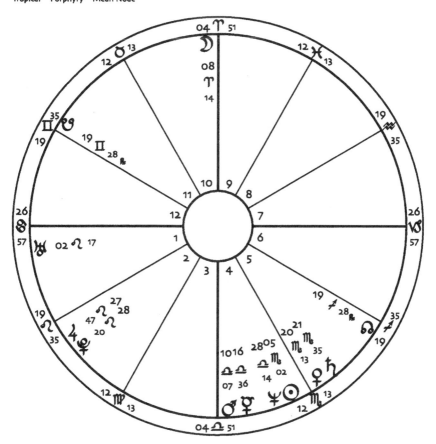

Stephen Curry

Natal Chart
March 14, 1988
1:51:00 PM EST
Akron, Ohio
41N05 / 81W31
Tropical   Porphyry   Mean Node

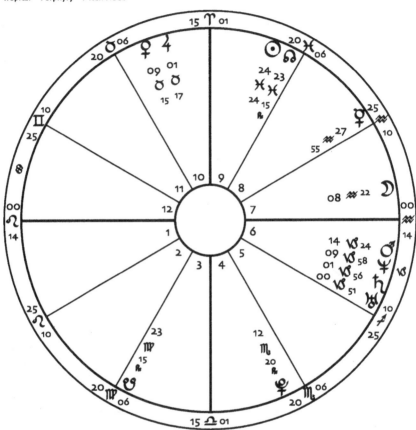

teacher, worked for three magazines (publishing), book author and publisher, and university professor. A woman with Saturn in Aquarius conjunct her descendant has been a partner in a group medical practice for 25 years, since her Saturn return.

According to Lunz, the 6th house should be examined next, including its dispositor and planets placed therein. He says the 6th house "governs employment, whereas the tenth is concerned with the nature of the occupation. In the horoscope of an employee the sixth house represents the employers. If and when he becomes an employer it then has reference to his employees."[43] In other words, the 6th house concerns the workplace or conditions of employment and situations of training where skills are developed, whereas the 10th house defines or influences our calling or ambitions, a sought-after social rank, status, or achievement. An example of this is Eddie, whose chart features Sun, Moon, Mercury, Venus, Mars, and Saturn in his 6th house. He's always at work, supervising a staff of over 120 employees. (See chart page 48.)

An unemployed man named David consulted me just before his second Saturn return. He'd been out of work for several years and was

David
Natal Chart
May 20, 1954
Tropical   Porphyry   Mean Node

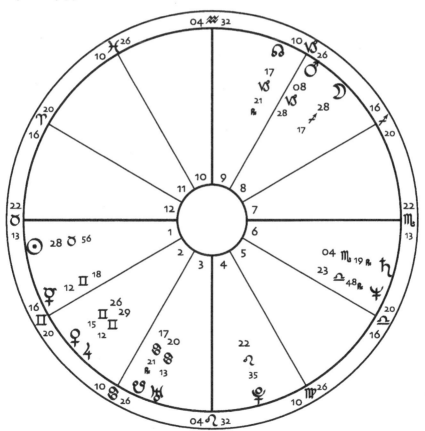

quite discouraged. Natally, he had Neptune and Saturn in the 6th house and transiting Saturn was currently conjunct natal Neptune, passing over it several times. He said his situation felt hopeless. It seemed that no one was interested in hiring a 58-year-old man without a college education. A recovering drug addict and alcoholic, sober for more than a decade, he was struggling with loss of faith. For someone with Saturn in the 6th house, being employed is very important to a sense of stability and security; it's a necessary component of the life structure. David had been working since age 15 (his first Saturn opposition) and had held innumerable jobs. I contemplated the meaning of natal Saturn in Scorpio in the 6th and asked if he'd ever done any work involving energy, chemistry or chemical reactions, given that Scorpio symbolizes transforming energies. I was just guessing here, using the symbolism to stimulate my intuition. He said he'd once worked for several years in a chemical factory. Keying on Saturn's conjunction with Neptune, I suggested that he apply to work at the local electrical and water utility companies, where the focus was on energy generation. I counseled him that during the remaining months of Saturn retrograde and its station near natal Neptune his situation might continue to be ambiguous, unclear, formless; it might take some time for things to clarify and take form, but nonetheless he could apply for positions. Referencing his Taurus Sun in the 1st house I believed he could project the identity of a reliable person, solidly built, with practical skills, a man who could be counted on. I suggested that he turn to the universe in an attitude of humility and spiritual devotion and approach the job search with a commitment to prayer, service, and discipleship, asking the universe to provide the sustenance he needed so he could be of service. This last comment, keyed on Saturn conjunct Neptune, was crucial, he told me, because it helped him surrender and maintain inner calm during several subsequent months of uncertainty. After Saturn turned direct in Libra and made its final pass over Neptune, he applied with the local electric and water utilities, got some interviews, but they kept him on hold for several months while nothing happened. When Saturn entered Scorpio and passed over natal Saturn for the first time he started working on a temporary basis. After Saturn turned direct in Scorpio, he was hired permanently by the water utility district, and within two years he was promoted three times. Recently, as Saturn entered Capricorn, he was promoted to a management position with increased salary and retirement benefits. David tells me that he has never forgotten the precise insights that astrology provided to guide his job search at a critical phase of life.

The next example highlights the 6th house / 10th house axis: Tony has Sun and Moon in the 6th house, trine Mars, Saturn, and Pluto in Leo in the 10th house. He has been working all his life, but his real

Tony
Natal Chart
April 8, 1948
Tropical   Koch   Mean Node

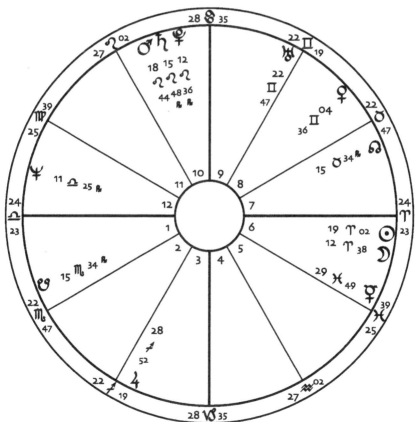

calling is fatherhood (Saturn in 10th). He loves his kids more than anything in life and he works to sustain them and launch them. He has natal Uranus in Gemini in the 9th house opposing Jupiter, he works as a software developer, and with Saturn squares his nodes, his work is grueling for a man nearing 70 years of age, but he applies himself with great discipline and commitment. His keynote is responsibility. His job is just his job, a means to pay the mortgage and college tuition. What he loves is sports, athletics, running, cycling, dance, and practicing Feldenkrais bodywork. Mars and Saturn square the nodes are expressed through attention to structural alignment and physical movement patterns.

Many vocational astrologers such as Noel Tyl examine the oriental planet, rising immediately before the Sun, and peregrine planets—unaspected—which tend to run away with the show. Tyl's Midheaven Extension Process examines the MC and its dispositor, and the chain of rulerships, until one reaches the final dispositor of the chart. One brief example of this technique: Picasso, working in varied material arts (four planets in Taurus), molded an entirely new vision of reality from his imagination: Saturn conjunct Neptune. Picasso's Midheaven ruler Mars is in Cancer and is governed by Moon in Sagittarius, which is disposited by Jupiter in Taurus, which is ruled by Venus in her home sign of Libra, sextile Moon in the 5th house of creativity—apt symbolism for a creative artist. Read Noel's book to integrate this midheaven extension technique.[44]

In vocational assessment, I place great emphasis on planets aspecting Sun and Moon, and their dispositors, as the following examples illustrate: Katrina has Sun-Mercury in her 9th house, Venus-Mars in Sagittarius at the MC, Jupiter trine the MC. Everything in her chart points to education, teaching, and intellectual life. She earned her doctorate in literature and then worked for ten years as an underpaid adjunct professor, while trying to get a full-time position. She finally landed a tenure track job when solar arc Saturn was conjunct natal Jupiter in her 2nd house. She stayed true to her natal pattern and worked her way up the ladder.

Wilson, a veterinarian, has Sun-Mercury conjunction in Scorpio

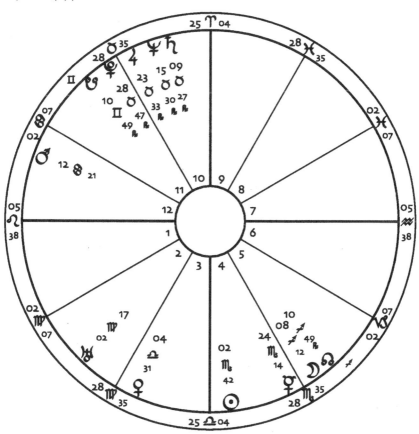

Pablo Picasso
Natal Chart
October 25, 1881
11:15:00 PM LMT
Málaga, Spain
36N43 / 4W25
Tropical   Porphyry   Mean Node

in the 1st house, closely squaring Pluto in the 10th house. He deals with animal emergencies, life and death situations, and performs surgery. The central career significator is the Sun, the Midheaven dispositor, placed in the 1st house, making him a prominent individual in his local community. With Sun conjunct Mercury, ruler of the 11th house, Wilson has spent much of his career as a member of a group veterinary practice (11th house: groups; Virgo: health care).

Denise, a gerontologist, owns a business, an in-home care for the elderly. She has Sun-Pluto conjunction in the 4th house in Leo. 4th house governs operating an establishment, a facility, a home.

Molly has Sun in Gemini opposite Saturn in Sagittarius and Moon in Capricorn in her 9th house. She earned degrees in French and linguistics (Gemini), then became a book editor for a major New York publisher (9th house). From 1989–91, when transiting Saturn and Uranus were conjunct her 9th house Moon, she experienced a sudden rise to a high position in the publishing industry.

Samantha, a chiropractor, has Chiron conjunct her Ascendant opposite the Sun; Mercury is conjunct Pluto in Virgo; she excels in

Katrina
Natal Chart
November 15, 1963
Tropical   Porphyry   Mean Node

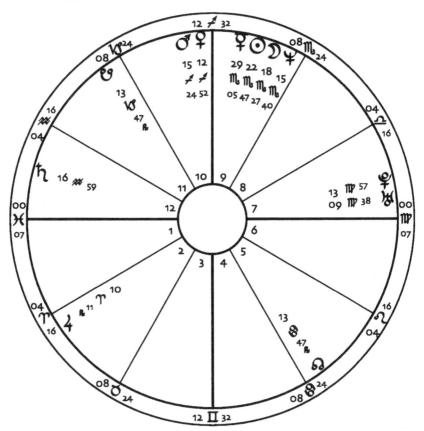

diagnostics. Sun trine Saturn in the 10th house signifies profession-alism, consistency, endurance, sustaining a medical practice over decades.

I also focus on planets contacting the nodal axis, as these are often accentuated. Stephen Curry has Ascendant ruler Sun conjunct the north node, which in this case indicates a superstar. Rupert Murdoch has Ascendant ruler Saturn in Capricorn, square the nodal axis and Uranus is conjunct the north node. These are symbols of his authority, social influence, and responsibility for a vast media empire. His Sun rules the 9th house of publishing and is conjunct Mercury, ruler of his

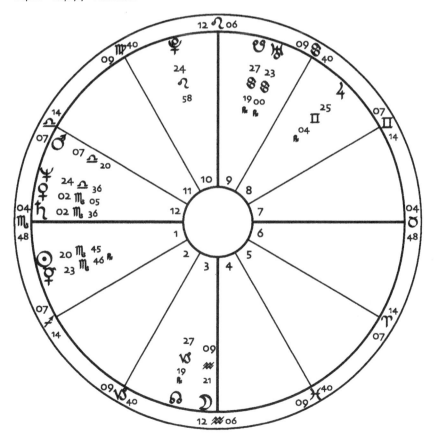

Wilson
Natal Chart
November 13, 1953
Tropical   Porphyry   Mean Node

Midheaven. Sun in house 4 often manifests as success later in life, after age 50.

Kelly, a major league professional athlete, experienced early career success followed by dissipation of potentials and a career-ending drug scandal. He has Mars conjunct south node in Aries; he was an amazing physical specimen, known for fiery, competitive, in-your-face play (Mars in Aries). Neptune opposes the Sun, squares the Ascendant, and is quincunx the Moon, as well as being involved in a grand trine in fire signs, showing his predilection for drugs and partying, and lapses of an athlete's self-discipline. After his career was over, a deep religious

Denise
Natal Chart
August 12, 1945
Tropical   Porphyry   Mean Node

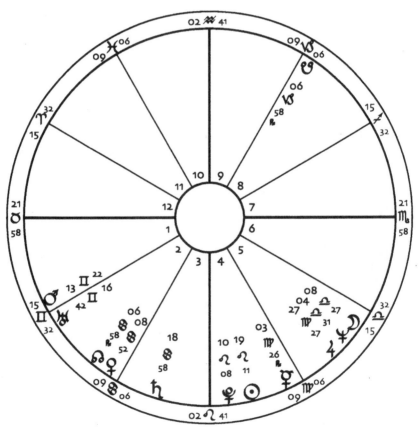

Molly
Natal Chart
June 3, 1958
Tropical   Porphyry   Mean Node

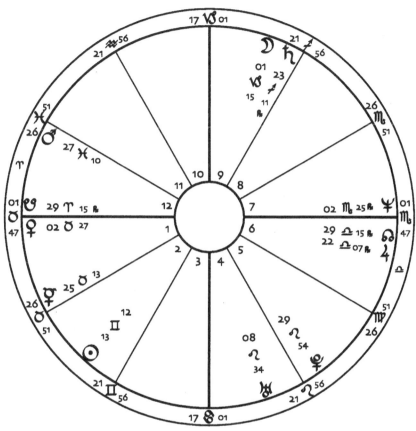

faith sustained him and he discovered a ministry that felt like his true purpose in life.

Another example pertaining to the nodes: Francesca was a few years past her first Saturn return but still hadn't settled on an occupational path. She had returned to school but was presently undecided on her college major. Transiting Saturn in Sagittarius was approaching a long conjunction to her natal Neptune at the cusp of the 9th house. She was very involved with spirituality and meditation, studying metaphysics and philosophy but now she needed to decide on something practical. She hoped that astrology could help her decide on a definite path.

Noting that she had Mars conjunct the nodal axis in Capricorn, trine her Ascendant I asked her if she was interested in athletics or competitive sports, and if she'd ever considered becoming a Physical Education teacher. She said, "I'm a very physical person. All my life I've been into athletics, training, fitness, yoga, and also somatic psychology. I can't think of anything I'd enjoy more than teaching yoga and martial arts and sports training to kids." Mars sextiles Mercury for strong, assertive verbal skills. A coach needs to bark out orders to her team. This intuitive suggestion emerging through astrological process work was reso-

Samantha
Natal Chart
Wednesday, August 20, 1958
Tropical Porphyry Mean Node

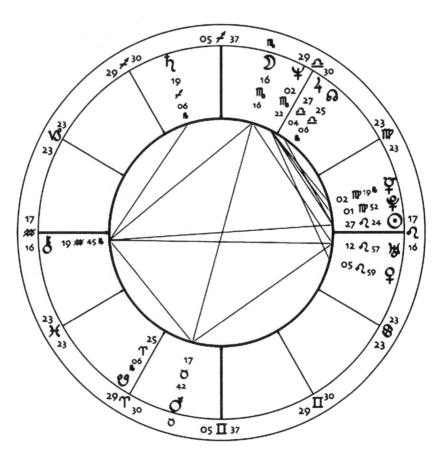

Rupert Murdoch

Natal Chart
March 11, 1931
11:59:00 PM AEST
Melbourne, Victoria
37S49 / 144E58
Tropical   Porphyry   Mean Node

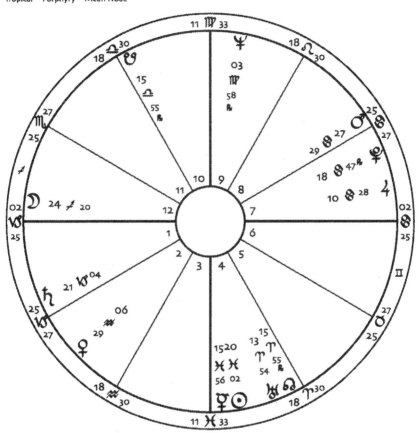

nant with her interests. As Saturn entered Capricorn, she shifted her college studies toward gaining the credentials she needed to pursue this career. I oriented her to the upcoming long transit of Pluto square natal Saturn and Pluto. She needed to get serious about her training and credentials, to be fully certified in various aspects of health psychology, to become more of an expert and authority on the subject.

Kelly
Natal Chart
May 21, 1977
Tropical   Porphyry   Mean Node

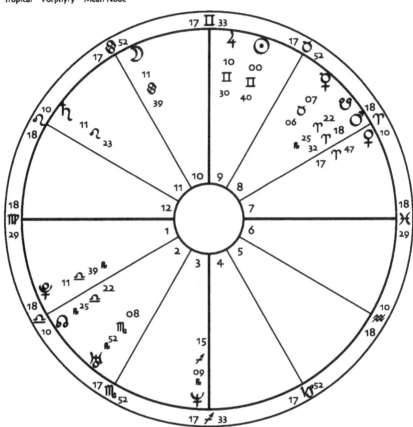

A Personal Anecdote About a Key Spiritual Lesson

These are some starting points for vocational astrology. But my goal here isn't to review all the rules for how to determine a person's occupation astrologically. There are several excellent books that do that, for example Faye Cossar-Blake's *Vocational Astrology: Finding the Right Career Direction*; and Judith Hill's *Vocational Astrology*.[45] However, I'm very Neptunian: I don't think well in a linear fashion, following a strict procedure for chart analysis. So, I want to discuss how my own approach has

Francesca
Natal Chart
November 7, 1982
Tropical   Porphyry   Mean Node

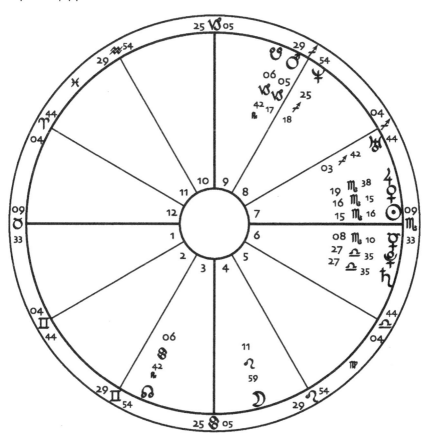

been evolving, beginning with this story about my very first contact with astrology, in 1978, when I was 20 years old. I met Chakrapani Ullal at the Siddha Yoga ashram and went to see him in Bombay, where he gave me an amazing reading, detailed in *Planets in Therapy*.

From my natal conjunction of Jupiter and Rahu, the north lunar node, Chakrapani correctly predicted I'd eventually become "a teacher, a lecturer, a counselor and advisor." This was before the idea of becoming an astrologer had ever crossed my mind. Then I remember him saying, "You will reach a high state of consciousness when you are 46 years old." What happened when I was 46 was this: The preceding two years was the time of my progressed Full Moon in Virgo, in the 12th house, and that progressed Full Moon squared my natal Mars and Saturn in Sagittarius. Simultaneously transiting Pluto was conjunct Mars and Saturn. Because the progressed Moon was in Virgo, there was emphasis on my experience as a worker, in the field of education (Sagittarius). My boss, who had been a professional mentor, abruptly turned against me and became critical and hostile. Everything I did was wrong. She wanted to promote another faculty member and decided to demote me from my position as graduate program director. I was quite upset about it, but managed to turn things around and continued teaching and held onto my job for a few years. But when my next contract renewal came up, I was offered a promotion in academic rank *and* a pay cut! Recently I'd stood in an airport bookstore browsing a book that I believe was titled *The Businessman Samurai* and I remember the first principle discussed was "Never accept a pay cut: Always resign." I thought about how I'd feel if I accepted the terms of that contract. My employers assumed I'd be desperate to maintain my job at all costs, no matter how hokey the deal was. They were also letting me know that it would be just fine with them if I left. In any event, that's how it made me feel. I realized that I was being treated as a line item in a budget, rather than as a person. So, after much deliberation I decided to call their bluff and quit. No one expected that. Interestingly enough, that program folded a few years later, after the school, following a similar strategy, drove out many of the older, experienced instructors and students left in droves. For me it felt like reaching a high state of consciousness to take a leap of faith and realize that I'd be okay, I'd survive, and I didn't deserve to be treated that way. I had enough self-respect to reject a contract with a pay cut. These are the kinds of tactics many organizations resort to nowadays. To reduce costs, they cut full-time jobs and add part-timers with no benefits and lower salaries. They target workers over 45 or 50 and try to get them to leave so younger, cheaper workers can take their place. This is a challenge for people in the *career maintenance* phase, as it interrupts the natural career cycle. This is the type of precarious envi-

*With Chakrapani at a pizza restaurant
on Geary Street, San Francisco, circa 2004.*

ronment many working people find themselves in nowadays, in a new corporate culture that utilizes ruthless management strategies reflecting the recent Uranus-Pluto square. Many people's occupational lives have been turned upside down by this.

Astrology can help us come to terms with this situation because we have an archetype that explains it—Pluto, the impersonal power principle. During Pluto transits it's not uncommon to encounter corruption, the assertion or abuse of power, and reptilian, cold-blooded actions or policies. Daggers come out. Pluto brings the awareness that it's a rough world out there; we have to be tough and resilient, to be survivors. Sometimes we're embattled. Around that time, I had a dream of myself wearing an animal skin, which carried the feeling that I'd been through trials, ordeals, and initiations. I learned that wearing an animal skin was a trait of the Greek god Dionysus, so in that light I decided to welcome the wild unruliness of the situation. And right at that moment I was recruited to teach at a different school across town, and start a graduate program that was in direct competition with my

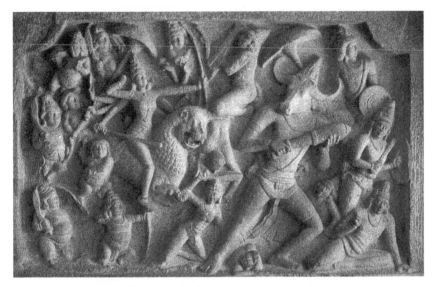

Battle of Durga and Mahisha, Mahisamardini Cave,
Mamallapuram, Tamil Nadu

former school's program, which, as I mentioned, folded several years later. Reflection on astrological symbolism helped me navigate a major career transition. With astrology's guidance we can develop a moving center, a center constantly in motion. It's especially important to understand that our secure life structures sometimes need to change, and predictably do so under the influence of transits of Pluto, Neptune, and Uranus to natal Saturn, which are some of the key transits for career crisis.

Career Crisis

Astrology is most helpful in understanding career crises and transitions. Crisis refers to a sudden, disorienting situation that's disruptive and causes consternation for the individual, and requires finding new ways of dealing with a problem that arises suddenly. Transits such as Uranus, Neptune, or Pluto aspecting natal Saturn are common indicators of career crisis because these transits challenge our structural security.

*Dionysus with a panther skin on his left arm, an ivy branch
in his left hand, and a spear or staff in the right hand.
Akragas (Agrigento), Sicily, circa 510 BCE.*

Bradley, age 62, is a highly skilled, credentialed corporate consultant and trainer. His chart features Saturn in Scorpio square Pluto in
the 4th house. Brad had rough experiences growing up with a violent,
tyrannical father, and in his adult life with several of his bosses, with
whom he had vehement disagreements and power struggles. When he
consulted me, Brad had been unemployed for three years since a trau-
matic event during his second Saturn return in the 6th house (house
of employment). At that time, he presented a report to the CEO and
the Board of Directors of a Fortune 500 company but his recommendations for organizational changes were rejected, he was fired by the
Board, and he lost standing (reputation) and a great deal of money. He
met inflexible authority, the archetype of the dictator. And he needed
me to hear that story. I noted that at the time of that crisis, his progressed Sun was conjunct his midheaven, and I asked him, "Did you do

your best on that report and in the way you stood behind your findings and recommendations? Did you give that CEO and board of directors the best professional advice you could give them at that moment?" Brad affirmed this. I said, "Then I think you've already achieved success, you did your job well. So why don't you stop beating yourself up about getting fired. It happens to everyone at some point. It has certainly happened to me." That was a crucial moment, when Brad felt empathically seen and validated. This set in motion the emotional release he needed to return to work, to get established again. Sometimes assignments come to an end and we need to disengage and move on. This is a spiritual perspective that emerges from consideration of astrological symbolism. Brad started a new job a few months later, when transiting Jupiter conjoined natal Saturn in his 6th house.

Trait and Factor Theory

Now let's explore how career counseling theories can enhance vocational astrology. The modern field of career counseling began in 1909 with Frank Parsons's book, *Choosing a Vocation*, which described "Trait and Factor Theory," which involves assessment of the characteristics of the person and the job. To select an occupation, Parsons said, you need a clear understanding of yourself—your attitudes, abilities, interests, ambitions, and resource limitations; and you need knowledge of the requirements and conditions of success, the advantages and disadvantages of occupations, the compensation, opportunities, and prospects in different lines of work. A wise choice is made by reasoning about the relations between self-knowledge and knowledge of the world of work. Career counseling begins with assessing the person's past achievements (including school grades, accomplishments in work), present abilities, and future aptitudes, and a person's interests, values, and personality traits. Typically, this is done through tests such as ACT: American College Testing and ASVAB: Armed Services Vocational Aptitude Battery. Interests are measured by the Strong Interest Inventory. Interests measured by the Strong test include: athletics; computer hardware and electronics; counseling and helping; culinary arts; entrepreneurship; finances and investing; healthcare services; human resources and

Bradley

Natal Chart
December 12, 1955
Tropical   Porphyry   Mean Node

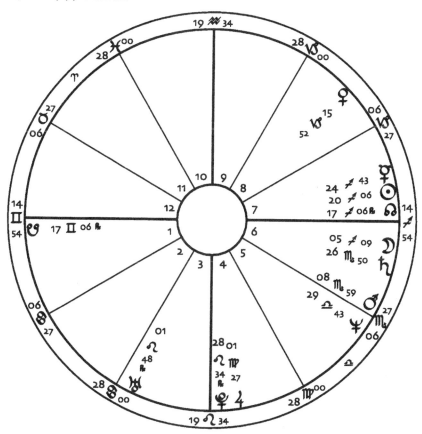

training; law; management; marketing and advertising; mathematics; mechanics and construction; medical science; military; nature and agriculture; office management; performing arts; politics and public speaking; programming and information systems; protective services; religion and spirituality; research, sales; science; social sciences; taxes and accounting; teaching and education; visual art and design; writing and mass communication.

Another test, the Kuder Career Search Interest Inventory, assesses these interests: agriculture, food, natural resources; architecture and construction; creative arts, audio-visual technology and communications; business management and administration; health science; hospitality and tourism; human services; information technology; law, public safety, corrections, and security; manufacturing; marketing; science, technology, engineering, mathematics; transportation, distribution and logistics.

It's a huge task to try to establish astrological correlates for each of these varied occupational categories. To make this task more manageable, in a few minutes I'll introduce the famous John Holland model, which conveniently organizes all of this into six broad categories of vocational interests and aptitudes.

The next stage of Trait and Factor career counseling involves obtaining knowledge about the world of work, gathering descriptions of various occupations, working conditions, salary, employment outlook, requirements for each occupation a person is considering. The best resource for this is called the Occupational Outlook Handbook, which describes hundreds of occupations. It's now called Occupational Information Network (o*net), and is available online for free. For each occupation, it describes *worker characteristics* (abilities, interests, work styles); *worker requirements* (skills, education, critical thinking, capacity for active learning); social skills such as persuading, negotiating, instructing, problem solving; technical abilities (testing, maintaining, repairing), judgment and decision-making; ability to manage time and resources. *Experience requirements*: such as relevant coursework, internship, or work experience; licenses, certificates. *Occupational requirements*: general types of work activities: information seeking, processing, and evaluating, problem solving, performing technical or physical work, communication with others. *Organizational contexts*: the way people do their work; amount of control over decision making that workers have; variety of skills used; autonomy; feedback and evaluation; recruitment and selection of employees; training and development; pay and benefits. *Work contexts*: methods of communication, job interactions, work setting, hazards, physical demands, challenges, pace and schedule of work. I believe all vocational astrologers can greatly benefit from making use of this informative database.

The final step in trait and factor counseling is matching the person's traits and factors with the world of work. Typically, computer guidance systems are used to combine tests and occupational information and self-assessments. Counseling involves moving between self-assessment and occupational info, making suggestions to the client, giving information about occupations.

This is where as astrologers we take a completely different approach, using the horoscope to try to match the person up to the right career. The great vocational astrologers such as Charles Lunz, Noel Tyl, Joanne Wickenburg, Judith Hill, and Faye Cossar-Blake make this process quite elegant, showing how to match vocational interests to planetary factors. In my own work I've tended to analyze how certain occupations are indicated based on a chart's zodiacal sign emphasis, and the Sun's sign, house placement, its dispositor, and planets aspecting the Sun. I utilize these as key vocational indicators. Sometimes the correlations are meaningful. For example, with planetary emphasis in Gemini, a person may prefer occupations emphasizing writing, speech, language or linguistics, communication. The famous storyteller and monologist, Spalding Gray, has Sun, Mercury, and Jupiter in Gemini. Poet Allen Ginsberg's chart is very similar, with Sun-Mercury in Gemini in the 3rd house, squaring the Moon.[46]

More than 30 years ago I did a chart for a young woman who had Sun-Venus-Mars in Cancer in the 4th house and was looking for a job. Because of this Cancer emphasis in her chart, I suggested she explore the fields of property and hotel management. She pursued it and over 30 years she moved up from front desk clerk to vice president of a major hotel chain. Somehow that suggestion seemed like an easy one. As another example, the sign of Leo is often linked to occupations involving drama, theatrical personality, performance, and self-expression. Actor Robert de Niro has Sun, Jupiter and Pluto in Leo, Sun conjunct north node (often a symbol of remarkable talent and solar charisma), and also Sun square Mars in Taurus—expressed through the kind of rough, cantankerous, pugnacious characters he has portrayed in films such as *Raging Bull, Midnight Run,* and *Meet the Fockers.*

Ellie, age 28 and approaching her first Saturn return, has risen at a

Spalding Gray

Natal Chart
June 5, 1941
1:51:00 AM EDT
Providence, Rhode Island
41N49 / 71W25
Tropical   Porphyry   Mean Node

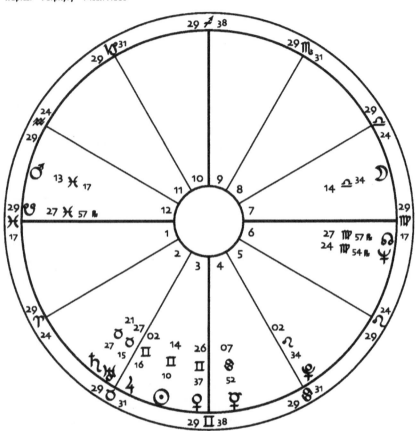

young age through the corporate ranks as a Human Resources manager overseeing many employees. Her chart features a conjunction of Saturn, Uranus, and Neptune in Capricorn in the 6th house of employment, benefits, and workplace dynamics. Preponderance in Capricorn suggests abilities in management and handling large responsibilities. Her early career ascent was timed by transiting Uranus in Aries and Pluto aspecting her natal Capricorn planets. She's also in charge of

Allen Ginsberg

Natal Chart
June 3, 1926
2:00:00 AM EDT
Newark, New Jersey
40N44 / 74W10
Tropical   Porphyry   Mean Node

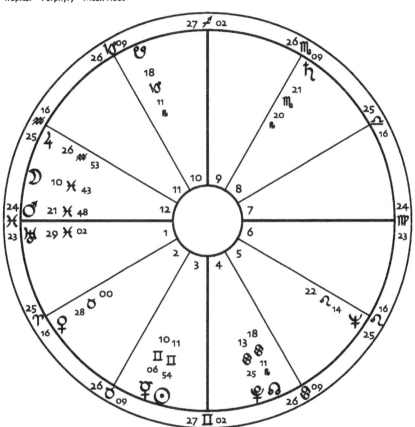

her company's diversity training, expressing Saturn conjunct Uranus, planet of social change.

Robert, an intellectual property lawyer, has Sun trine Jupiter, planet of law, and his Moon in Sagittarius opposite Jupiter, with Moon and Jupiter both squaring Mars-Saturn in the 9th house in Pisces.

Tricia, a professional baker (specializing in wedding cakes) for over 35 years, has Venus (ruler of sweets and weddings) at her MC, con-

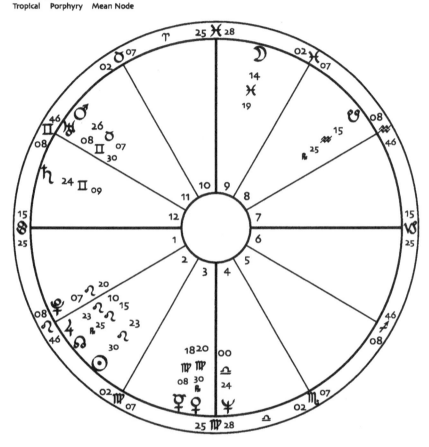

Robert de Niro
Natal Chart
August 17, 1943
3:00:00 AM EWT
Brooklyn, New York
40N38 / 73W56
Tropical   Porphyry   Mean Node

junct Mars. Her Virgo Moon is in the 4th house opposite Mars; baking requires much physical energy and exertion. With her Capricorn Sun in the 8th house, opposite Uranus, she has always been independent, managing her own business since she was 30.

These examples illustrate how some people have relatively clear occupational signatures. But I've also found that the correlations of astrological signs and houses to specific occupations aren't always clear

Ellie
Natal Chart
August 31, 1989
Tropical   Porphyry   Mean Node

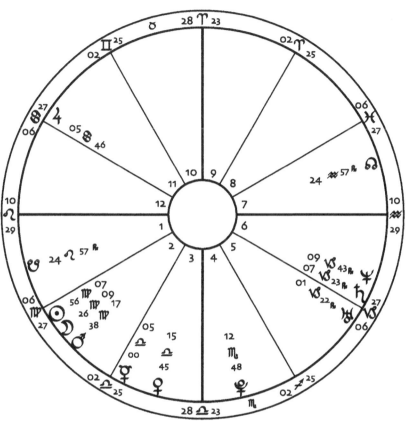

and obvious. For example, natal emphasis in Aries (Sun in Aries or several planets in this sign) or a prominent natal Mars could be expressed through any occupation requiring initiative, motivation, energy, assertiveness, and self-directedness. That's too vague to really be helpful, as it can apply to an almost infinite number of occupations. And even though Taurus and the 2nd house signify money, not everyone in the fields of accounting, banking, or financial services has strong planetary emphasis in this sign or house. Virgo and the 6th house signify health and health care, but not all medical professionals have Virgo or 6th

Robert
Natal Chart
February 14, 1966
Tropical   Porphyry   Mean Node

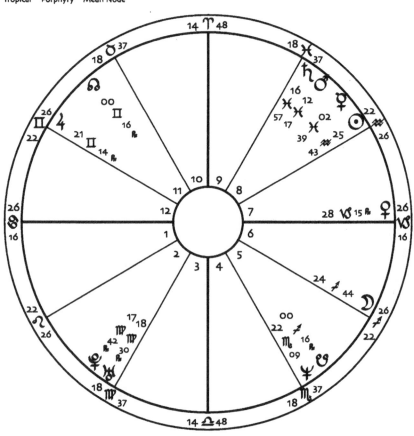

house planets. The reality is that people with all kinds of planetary and zodiacal emphasis enter various occupations.

Let's look at the chart of Laura, who has Sun in Pisces in the 12th house, and four planets, Uranus, Saturn, Mars, Neptune, in Capricorn in her 10th house. Laura works in the field of health care administration for a large insurance brokerage. She has been in the health industry since college graduation. At first glance her chart doesn't immediately highlight health care. The symbolism of Pisces and the 12th house implies work with hospitals or social services. Her Capricorn,

Tricia
Natal Chart
January 4, 1953
Tropical   Porphyry   Mean Node

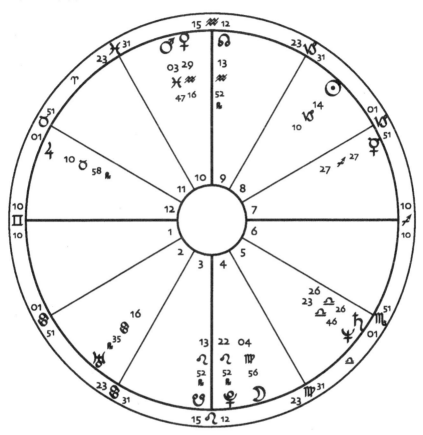

10th house planets suggest the potential for some executive or admin-
istrative, professional role, and it's not surprising that she has spent her
entire career working in corporate environments. Arguably, the south
node in Virgo denotes diligence in a service role related to health care.
Mercury in Aquarius in the 11th house signifies her keen interest in her
field and active role in conferences and professional meetings. Pluto in
Scorpio in the 8th house suggests an investigative component, referring
to that part of her job carried out in collaboration with actuaries, who
estimate people's life spans. Pluto in the 8th house concerns the finan-

Laura
Natal Chart
March 6, 1988
Tropical   Porphyry   Mean Node

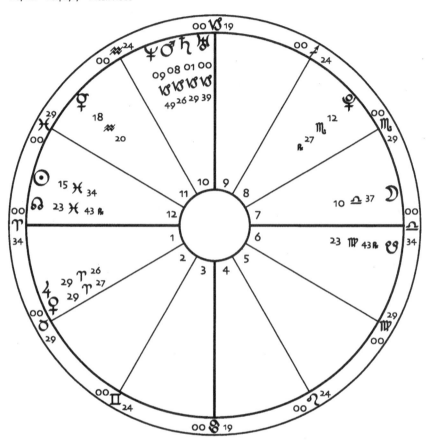

cial agreements that insurance implies—the system of payments and
reimbursements, the trust between individuals and institutions. But I
wouldn't have been able to guess this precise occupation from her birth
chart. I have to admit that I can't always easily identify the best, most
appropriate career for someone. While I can't promise a client absolute
certainty that I can specify a precisely matched vocational choice indicated in the chart, I've developed confidence that a process-oriented
approach is likely to uncover unexpected insights, to reveal the innate
archetypal pattern that is striving to be realized. The story of Francesca
discussed earlier is a good illustration of this.

Lifespan Career Perspective

Now let's discuss the idea of a lifespan perspective on career development. For astrologers, attunement to the cycles of Saturn is a key to our analysis of life cycles, which is essential for career counseling. Vocational psychologist Donald Super said that careers develop in five stages across the lifespan: *growth* (of capacities and interests in childhood and adolescence; typically at our first Saturn opposition), *exploration* (of possibilities, information-seeking about various jobs, job-hunting—typically in early adulthood at our Saturn ¾ square, our Saturn return, or at later stages), *establishment* (getting started and established in an occupation), *maintenance* (sustaining a job or career path over time), and *disengagement* (retirement or unemployment, when you must let go and move forward). All of these phases can be linked to important phases of the Saturn cycle insofar as it governs slow establishment and maintenance of life structures.

Doris, chancellor of a large city's Public Schools district, told me, "I don't want to do that job anymore." She was burned out, exhausted, wanted to test the waters and see about finding a new job. Noting that she was 54 years old and that transiting Saturn was in her 2nd house, opposing Sun in the 8th house, I recommended that she make the most practical, realistic decision possible, and I asked what might that be. Doris informed me that her pension would be fully vested in just two more years. I asked, "Wouldn't your overall position be stronger if you stay on the job until you reach that point of earning your full pension? Then you can do whatever you want!" That fit the meaning of transiting Saturn opposite Sun—making a pragmatic decision, supporting career maintenance, but also planning for the upcoming stage of disengagement.

The Life Space and Role Salience

Donald Super also described the "life space," the idea that our work role isn't our only role in life. Over the course of time, our major roles include child, student, worker, spouse and home-maker, citizen, and leisurite. Each of us gives different importance to school (or self-education), work, home, family, community involvement, and leisure. Super uses the term *role salience*: the degree of one's participation, commitment, and the value placed on our roles in these six areas. Astrology expands our vision of the life space, through considering the 12 houses. Astrologically, Super's realm of school and the student role corresponds to 3rd and 9th houses. Work corresponds to the 6th and 10th houses. Home and family spheres correlate with the 4th house. Community involvement is found in the 11th house. Leisure activities are linked to the 5th house. But this leaves out houses 1, 2, 8, 9, and 12. Considering all 12 houses expands our view of the life space. House 1 is the realm of

Doris
Natal Chart
June 18, 1962
Tropical   Porphyry   Mean Node

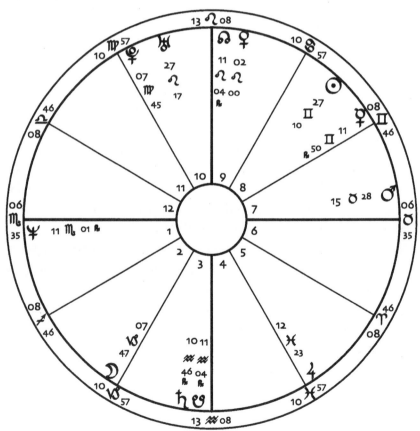

self-image, persona, and the body, our visible appearance and behavior. House 2 is the sphere of personal finances and ownership—clearly a distinct sphere of our life space. House 3 corresponds to school, learning, and also mobility and transportation. House 4 governs family dynamics, but also the physical location and conditions of the home, house, or property. House 5 represents children, as well as play, leisure, and creativity. House 6 is the domain of work, training, and apprenticeship, but also health and self-improvement, which can be central concerns of a person's life space. House 7 governs friendships, spousal relationships and marriage. House 8 is the realm of sexuality, shared finances, business, investment, and interpersonal commitments. House 9 is the realm of travel, adventure, education, teaching, religion and philosophy, forming concepts and theories to define life's meaning. House 10 relates to one's career or professional role. House 11 is the domain of group membership, community involvement, and social activism. House 12 is the realm of spirituality, dreams, solitude, and inner life. Astrologers can expand Super's model through our understanding that, based on their birth pattern, people vary in the emphasis they place on involvement in these areas of their life space. We can find salience in our involvement in multiple spheres of life, and move our attention intelligently through different realms as our transits change.

Vocational Astrology and the John Holland Typology

Now let's look at the most widely utilized and researched career counseling models, John Holland's model of vocational types. Holland assigns people's vocational interests and work environments to six categories: *conventional, investigative, realistic, enterprising, social,* and *artistic.* These are measured by Vocational Preference Inventory (VPI) and Self-Directed Search (SDS), tests that measure self-perceived competencies and interests. Holland describes six work environments and the personality type of the person who matches that environment. Where Holland speaks of vocational interests and environments, I also refer to vocational capacities.

Conventional work involves skill in maintaining systems, following established procedures, administration, managing budgets and information systems. The conventional work environment is characterized by organization and planning, such as offices where one needs to keep records, file papers, organize reports. It may involve bookkeeping, accounting, word processing, data processing, calculating. Here one needs clerical skills and numerical ability, ability to organize, dependability, and ability to follow directions. The conventional personality type values money, dependability, following rules, orders, and guidelines. Most business entrepreneurs, including very artistic, creative people, require some degree of conventional work abilities to succeed in their enterprises.

I link conventional interests and capacities to strong placement or aspects of Saturn, such as Sun-Saturn aspects, which can signify a responsible, dependable, organized, conscientious person. Ellen, with a Sun-Saturn conjunction in her 9th house, is an Episcopal Priest, the only clergy person in charge of a large urban diocese. She works long hours to get the institutional work done. She performs the liturgy, leading public worship services. Her responsibilities include administration, coordinating committees, building and maintenance issues, Bible study, writing and delivering sermons, performing services, tending the flock. At age 15 Ellen became an evangelical Christian. With transiting Saturn opposite natal Sun-Saturn in the 9th house, she formed passionate convictions about religious doctrine and faith. Her work involves marking passages, guiding people through states of grief and bereavement (Scorpio Sun-Saturn, and Mars-Neptune in the 8th house). With Venus conjunct her midheaven, Ellen also exhibits social vocational interests in that she enjoys interacting with people, supporting and teaching them through private counseling and spiritual direction; moreover, she's an artist. She thus combines conventional, social, and artistic vocational interests.

Another example of someone who does predominantly conventional work is Richard, who has made a strong recovery from schizophrenia after he became seriously ill during the 1980s, when transiting Saturn and Pluto in Scorpio were conjunct his natal Neptune in the 12th house. At that time he became delusional, heard voices, and committed a violent crime that landed him in prison for a year (12th house). Pluto, ruler of his Scorpio Ascendant, planet of alchemical transformation, is at his midheaven. Richard is a chemist and his work involves meticulous rigor in laboratory methodology. With Jupiter in Sagittarius he's highly intelligent, religiously devout, and scrupulously ethical in his actions. His Virgo Sun is conjunct north node; he's the consummate hard worker, in a field at the interface of health care, science, and manufacturing. Venus is placed in his 11th house. He works for a scientific organization and is beloved within that company. With Sun in Virgo trine Saturn in Capricorn, he's a project manager and quality assurance specialist who supervises a large staff and looks after the details, the credentialing, the frequent laboratory audits. He exemplifies Virgo impeccability and Saturnian consistency. He makes sure all proper scientific procedures and government regulations are stringently followed. With Uranus square the Ascendant, he's an unusual person, a dedicated scientist, and excellent at programming computers and repairing networks.

Holland's *realistic* types have vocational interests that involve working with tools and machinery, skills in building, technical projects, repair and maintenance. The realistic work environment is physically demanding. The work setting has tools, machines, or animals. The worker must have technical competencies to fix machines or electronic equipment, drive cars or trucks, or herd animals. Examples include construction sites, auto garages, factories. Some realistic environments require physical agility or strength, such as roofing, outdoor painting, pipe fitting, plumbing, electrical and automotive repair, farming. The environment may be hazardous or produce more illness or accidents than other work environments. The realistic personality type is likely to enjoy using tools or machines. These individuals have little tolerance for abstract and theoretical pursuits. I link realistic vocational interests to strong placement or aspects of Mars, Saturn, or Uranus, such as aspects of the Sun to Mars, Saturn, or Uranus.

Abe is a carpenter and handyman. This is his noon chart, so just look at the planets; ignore the houses. He loves to work with tools and fix things. He has natal Sun-Mars conjunction, opposite Jupiter in Taurus, showing the physical strength and exertion required in his

Ellen
Natal Chart
November 21, 1955
Tropical Porphyry Mean Node

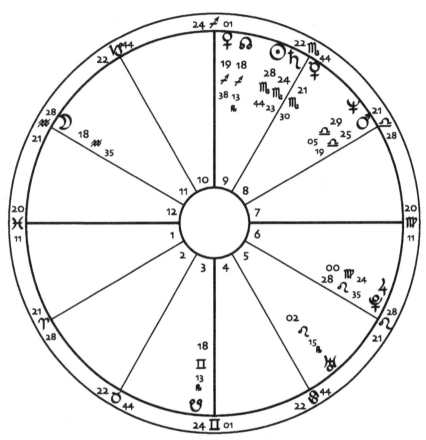

work. Mars-Jupiter aspects generally indicate vitality and vigor. Uranus is conjunct his north node. Abe has interests in electronics and is
developing skills as an electrician. The realistic type can be Uranian
insofar as the work involves science, technology, experiment, discovery, and electricity. His Mars in Scorpio is also semi-square Pluto. With
Sun and Mars square Saturn, Abe struggles with depression and low
self-esteem, stemming from not being seen, celebrated, and cheered on
by his father, also a carpenter, who died when Abe was eight (at Abe's

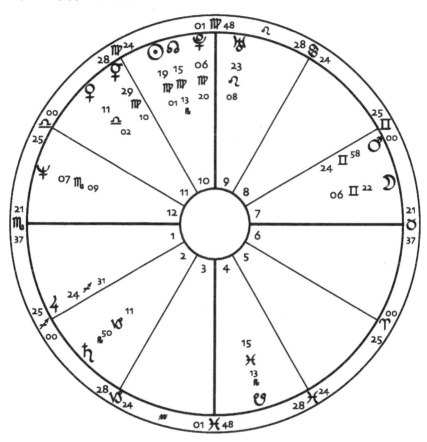

Richard
Natal Chart
September 11, 1960
Tropical Porphyry Mean Node

first Saturn square). The Sun wants acknowledgment, to be validated and mirrored by somebody, and Abe was starved for that (Sun square Saturn). With Sun opposite Jupiter, Abe reads books on philosophy, and is good with mathematics (Uranus-node), even though he didn't finish college. At age 49 he experienced career expansion when he had a business card made to promote his services and began distributing them, which showed emergence of what Holland calls enterprising vocational interests and capacities.

The *enterprising* type enjoys business, promotion, marketing, sales, persuasion, social leadership. In enterprising work environments, people manage and persuade others to attain organizational or personal goals. Persuasion and selling take place. Finance and economic issues are of prime importance. Enterprising people are generally self-confident, sociable, and assertive. Promotion and power are important. They often work in sales, buying, business management, politics, real estate, stock market, purchasing and trading goods and assets, insurance, or political lobbying. Enterprising people seek status and wealth. They like to use verbal skills to sell, persuade, or motivate. Assertive and popular, they gravitate to leadership positions. They prefer to persuade and manage, rather than to help others—which is the attitude of the social type.

Enterprising vocational pursuits typically engage the communication skills of Mercury, and the groundedness of Saturn; no enterprise runs well without the conventional work—the accounting, filing, record keeping, keeping things organized. Enterprising vocational pursuits (selling, persuading, leading) also require the energy and motivation of Mars, and are most successful when one can emanate the warmth, magnetism, and appealing confidence of the Sun, which makes it possible to successfully announce oneself and sell a product, an idea, a cause. In my opinion, aspects of Sun-Mars, Sun-Jupiter, or Mars-Jupiter indicate the capacity to spur on an enterprise and promote it enthusiastically. The question is whether one can do this without seeming pushy, obnoxious, and egotistical.

Martha Stewart has Sun in Leo conjunct Pluto, square the Ascendant, near the midheaven, a symbol of prominence. Sun is sextile Jupiter. She exudes self-confidence and clearly exemplifies the enterprising vocational interest. Martha takes pride in marketing her version of excellence. Moon in the 2nd house represents her interest in developing and selling home products. Venus square Jupiter represents the pursuit of style, beauty, and luxury.

Let's look at the chart of Amazon CEO Jeff Bezos. Because we have no confirmed birth time we'll use a Noon chart. Bezos has a Sun-Mars conjunction in Capricorn, apt symbolism for ambition and a drive for

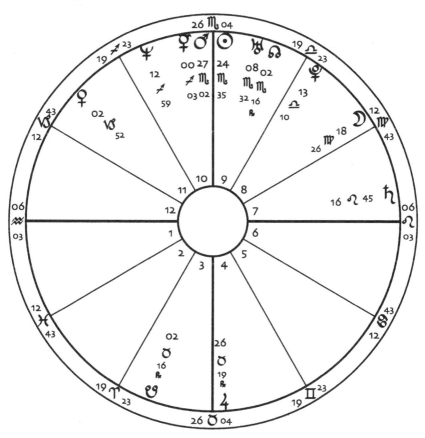

Abe
Natal Chart
November 16, 1976
Tropical   Porphyry   Mean Node

success. He also has Mercury conjunct south node in Capricorn, squaring Jupiter in Aries, symbolizing executive skill and intelligence in business management, and the expansive international scope of his enterprise. Jupiter in Aries square the nodal axis gives Bezos the impetus to initiate innovations in business and marketing that have come to dominate the world of online sales. Mercury's placement conjunct the south node, semi-square Saturn, and square Jupiter signifies business acumen and the emphasis on shipping and transportation. His Sun trines Pluto in Virgo; he's a man who holds the power—Sun-Pluto at its best. He

Martha Stewart
Natal Chart
August 3, 1941
1:33:00 PM EDT
Jersey City, New Jersey
40N44 / 74W05
Tropical   Porphyry   Mean Node

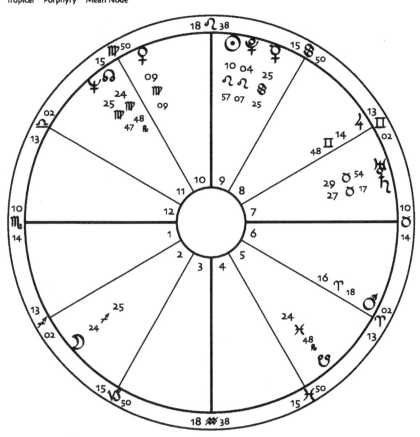

manages a vast empire. Regarding Bezos's vast wealth, his Venus-Saturn conjunction represents discipline and diligence in accumulating assets, but also note that Venus is exactly semi-square (45°) Jupiter. Jupiter-Venus is the planetary pair that symbolizes wealth and luxury. Larry Ellison, another billionaire, has a Venus-Jupiter conjunction in Virgo.

Enterprise at its best is about innovation—selling or promoting products and ideas that can change or improve the world, society,

Jeff Bezos
Natal Chart
January 12, 1964
12:00:00 PM MST
Albuquerque, New Mexico
35N05 / 106W39
Tropical   Porphyry   Mean Node

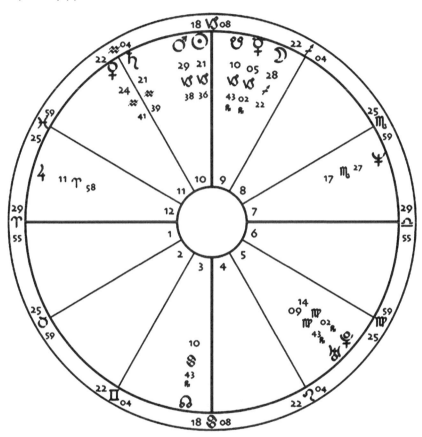

or the individual consumer. Thus, enterprise is often quite Uranian. People with prominent placement or aspects of Uranus often pursue unconventional, independent occupations involving new trends in culture, science, technology, media, or social change. Steve Jobs, a genius of enterprising business activity, had Pisces Sun exactly sesquiquadrate Jupiter and Uranus in Cancer.

Let's return to the chart of Phil, which I discussed in Chapter 2

Larry Ellison

Natal Chart
August 17, 1944
12:00:00 PM EWT
New York, New York
40N43 / 74W00
Tropical   Porphyry   Mean Node

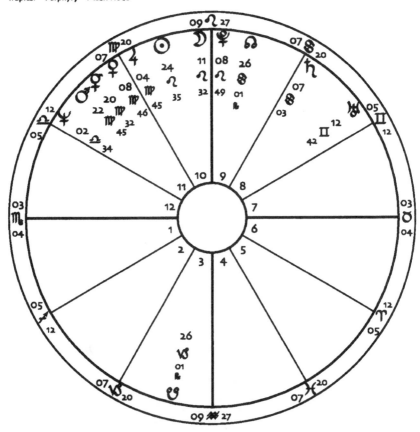

(chart on page 35). Jupiter in Virgo sextiles his Cancer Sun. And Uranus and Pluto in his 1st house square Mercury in Gemini in the career 10th house. He's a hard worker (Jupiter in Virgo), involved with new media and computer technology (Uranus-Pluto), writing and promoting software products (enterprising abilities). He also has artistic interests and abilities, employed in his roles as a web designer, part-time DJ and drummer (Sun-Venus-Mars conjunction). He's constantly engaged

Steve Jobs
Natal Chart
February 24, 1955
7:15:00 PM PST
San Francisco, California
37N47 / 122W25
Tropical   Porphyry   Mean Node

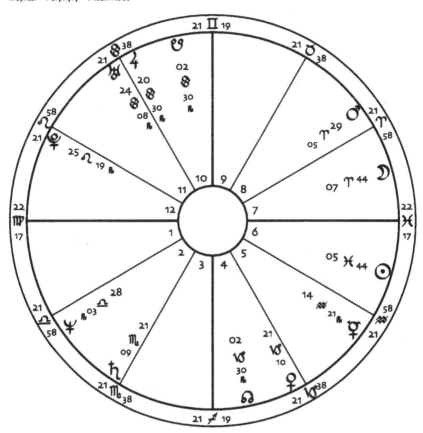

in learning (Mercury conjunct Midheaven), demonstrating investigative interests and capacities.

Holland's *investigative* type enjoys learning, inquiry, research,
scholarship, journalism or scientific investigation. This encompasses
research and investigative skills necessary in the practice of law and
law enforcement, medicine, and all fields of scientific inquiry. In investigative work environments people search for solutions to problems

through mathematical or scientific interests and competencies. People use complex and abstract thinking to solve problems creatively. This can include computer programmers, mathematicians, statisticians, biologists, science teachers, physicians, veterinarians, research and development managers. Individuals need to use logic and precise thinking to solve problems. It's not necessary for them to use human relations skills or to use machines. The investigative personality type enjoys learning, reading, writing, editing, solving puzzles and other challenges requiring use of intellect. They're not likely to enjoy supervising others or dealing with other people's personal problems; that's the strength of the social type.

Strong placement or aspects of Mercury generally show investigative interests and skills—for example the conjunction of Sun-Mercury, showing a highly verbal, thinking, communicative person. Investigative journalist Matt Taibbi has Mercury in Aquarius in a Yod with Mars in Aries and Pluto in Virgo as well as a Jupiter-Saturn opposition. Jon Stewart has Sun conjunct Mercury in Sagittarius, closely square Jupiter in Pisces, and squaring Uranus and Pluto. He writes and thinks brilliantly, with humor, intelligence, moral depth, and social impact. Sun-Mercury square Uranus represents Stewart's identity as a political satirist, activist, and sly commentator. Mercury square Pluto represents a deep thinker, analyst, critic, investigator. Stewart also has Sun sextile Saturn; he's a hard worker, and gave consistently great performances over years on television—a testament to his self-discipline. Over the course of his career there was no scandal, no lapse in his productivity.

One of our leading investigative journalists, Rachel Maddow, has Moon-Mercury in the 9th house, square Saturn in Gemini; she's a policy and information junkie, very loquacious, perceptive, and witty. Her Sun opposite Pluto and Uranus is expressed through tough, incisive commentaries on the world's forces of social change and influence. Also note how her Sun squares the Moon's nodes, often a symbol of prominence or having your face and your identity known in the world.

Another facet of the investigative type stems from the influence of Pluto, bringing the interests in research in fields as varied as criminal justice, study of genealogies, epidemiology, criminology, immunology,

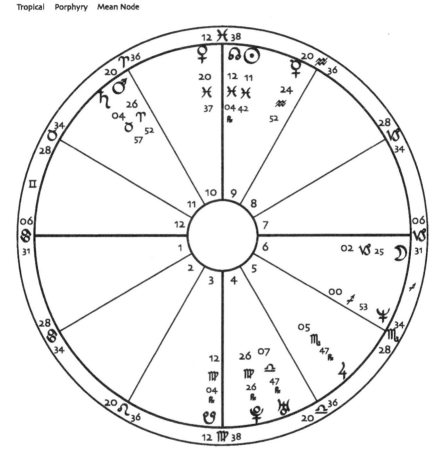

Matt Taibbi
Natal Chart
March 2, 1970
12:00:00 PM EST
Boston, Massachusetts
42N22 / 71W04
Tropical   Porphyry   Mean Node

forensic pathology, forensic accounting, or investigating paranormal phenomena, mysteries, and world conspiracies.

Here's another example of the investigative type: Jennifer, age 51, was born with Mercury rising, Capricorn Sun near the Ascendant, Sun-dispositor Saturn in the 3rd house (house of learning and communication), opposing Uranus and Pluto. She has graduate degrees in the field of Informatics, information science, and she's also an advanced

Jon Stewart
Natal Chart
November 28, 1962
12:00:00 PM EST
Trenton, New Jersey
40N13 / 74W45
Tropical   Porphyry   Mean Node

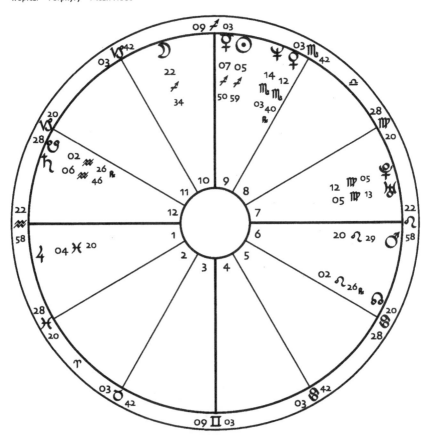

practice nurse (Jupiter in the 6th house). With Capricorn Sun sextile Saturn, she's a conscientious person who does computer system design, maintaining health records for a federal agency handling Veteran's health care (Saturn in Pisces, and Neptune in the 11th house). Her work combines conventional and investigative capacities; born on a Full Moon in Cancer, she enjoys being supportive in her nursing practice, showing social vocational interests.

According to Holland, the *artistic* type enjoys creative self-expression, being on stage, performing, creating, exhibiting, or composing

Rachel Maddow
Natal Chart
April 1, 1973
12:23:00 PM PST
Hayward, California
37N40 / 122W05
Tropical   Porphyry   Mean Node

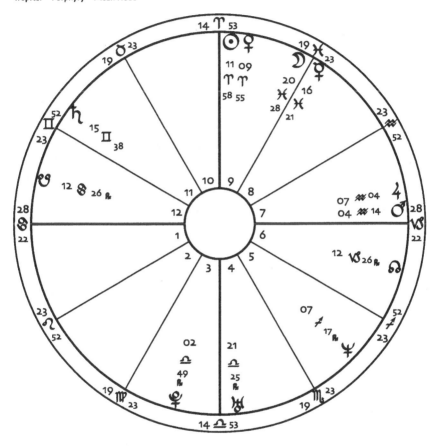

in artistic media. The artistic work environment is free and open, and encourages creativity and personal expression. This is the realm of the musician, fine artist, creative writer, actor/actress, dancer, film director. Here people can dress how they wish, and structure their own time. Tools are used for self-expression rather than to complete a task. The artistic type likes to express herself by creating music, art, or writing. This type values originality and creativity.

Sun signifies the courage and confidence and strong solar emanation needed to project oneself publicly in both enterprising and artistic

Jennifer
Natal Chart
January 7, 1966
Tropical   Porphyry   Mean Node

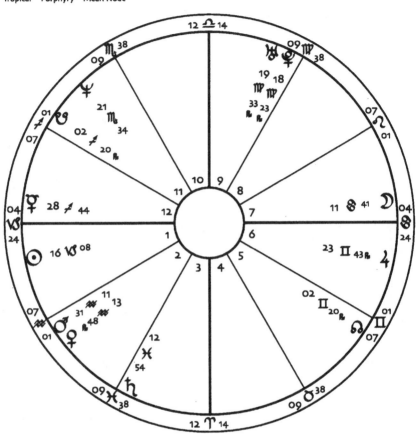

avenues. Artistic people benefit from the energy of Mars, as it represents motivation and assertiveness needed for success in artistic projects. Uranus gives originality, uniqueness, and freedom of self-expression. But artistic traits are most reflective of strong placement or aspects of Venus, especially aspects of Venus-Sun, Venus-Mercury, Venus-Mars, Venus-Jupiter, Venus-Uranus, and Venus-Neptune. For example, David (discussed earlier in this chapter), with Venus-Jupiter conjunct in Gemini opposite the Moon and trine Neptune, is a drummer who plays in rock, jazz, and R&B bands. As I'll note in Chapter 6, the charts of many musical and artistic individuals such as Jimi Hendrix, Bonnie Raitt, and Elvis Presley feature conjunction or semi-square of Sun-Venus.

Joni Mitchell's Moon at the MC opposes Venus and Neptune at the IC, symbolizing her delicate voice, her journeys of imagination and songs of emotional ordeals, her romantic agonies and quest for spiritual redemption, and her music's soulful celebration of the space of feminine solitude, as well as pleasure and delight in experience.

Actress Scarlett Johansson has Venus conjunct Jupiter and Neptune. Her palpable magnetism and sex appeal stems from three planets in Scorpio, including Pluto square Mars.

The life story of actor Morgan Freeman is fascinating. As a child growing up in rural Tennessee, he encountered an environment that featured Jim Crow laws, systematic racism, and segregation. His natal Sun semi-squares Pluto, planet of bigotry and hatred. Freeman's Sun squares Neptune, and his Sun is conjunct the Moon's south node. His Sun also semi-squares Venus, symbol of a loving, affable man and a refined, artistic personality. His Sun-Venus-Pluto alignments represent the way Freeman emanates inner beauty that stems from facing suffering and adversity and rising up to overcome it. His chart features Jupiter in the 10th house, opposing Pluto, sesquare (135° aspect) the Sun. He carries an air of humility, integrity, spiritual nobility, and elevation of character. With a Sun-Jupiter sesquare, Freeman has come to embody the identity of a kind and wise man. With Venus rising, he has a beautiful face. Venus squares Jupiter and forms a T-Square to Pluto. Apparently, he's ranked as the fifth-highest earning box office star with $4.31 billion in total box office gross earnings, an average of $74.4 million per film. Venus-Jupiter aspects are associated with wealth, and here Pluto powerfully boosts this effect.

It's important to note that Freeman did not succeed in his acting career at first. At the age of 30, in 1967, he caught a break as a cast member in an all African-American Broadway production of *Hello, Dolly*. He married his first wife that same year. This was his first Saturn return, and also transiting Saturn in Aries was conjunct his Ascendant. He gained his first national exposure beginning in 1971 while appearing

Joni Mitchell
Natal Chart
November 7, 1943
10:00:00 PM MWT
Fort Macleod, Alberta
49N43 / 113W25
Tropical   Porphyry   Mean Node

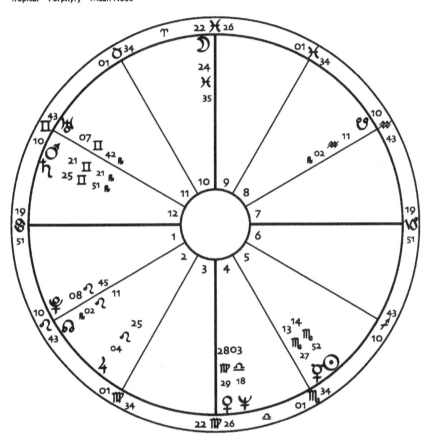

on *The Electric Company*, a TV show that taught children how to read. Transiting Saturn in Taurus was conjunct Mercury-Uranus in Taurus in his 2nd house; presumably he honed his communication skills and started earning some steady money. Uranus in Libra was conjunct his Descendant, signifying a greater impact on the public and significant new alliances. By 1976 this TV show was cancelled and Morgan hit a rough patch in his life. He couldn't get the big movie roles he wanted and his marriage was falling apart. Transiting Saturn in Cancer was

Scarlett Johansson
Natal Chart
November 22, 1984
7:00:00 AM EST
New York, New York
40N43 / 74W00
Tropical   Porphyry   Mean Node

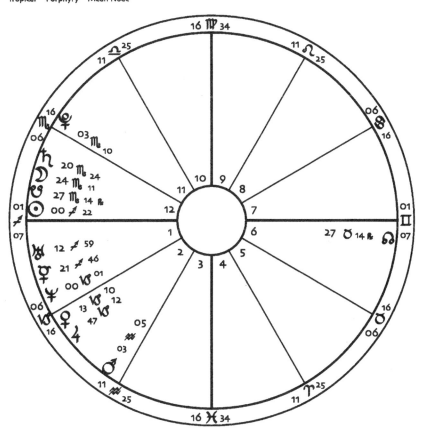

conjunct natal Pluto, squaring Venus, and opposing his 10th house Jupiter, indicating a period of adversity in marriage and professional life. At the same time as Saturn was conjunct natal Pluto, transiting Pluto in Libra began a long pass over his Descendant, showing a phase of descent, defeat of the ego, and difficult endings. With his divorced finalized in 1979 he found himself alone and began to drink too much. Transiting Saturn was conjunct Neptune in his 6th house.

In 1984 he married for a second time and adopted the grand-

Morgan Freeman
Natal Chart
June 1, 1937
2:00:00 AM CST
Memphis, Tennessee
35N09 / 90W03
Tropical   Porphyry   Mean Node

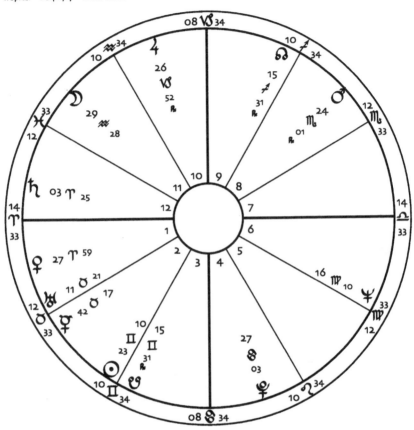

daughter of his first wife. At this time, transiting Pluto in Scorpio formed a quincunx to natal Saturn (adjusting to parental role); Uranus in Sagittarius opposed his Sun, ruler of the 5th house, signifying forming a relationship with a child; and Jupiter in Capricorn passed over his Midheaven. Freeman had some small successes in TV shows until 1987, when he landed a role in the film *Street Smart*. In the late 1980s, transiting Saturn, Uranus, and Neptune came into conjunction at his Midheaven. From there his career began to take off. His acclaimed film history includes *Bruce Almighty*, *Shawshank Redemption*, *Driving Miss Daisy*, *The Bucket List* and many more. By the time he was in his mid-sixties he was at the peak of his fame. At that time, transiting Neptune passed over natal Jupiter, squaring Venus. Pluto trined his natal Saturn, representing gaining the world's deep respect. Freeman worked constantly in the film industry, with hit after hit. His beautiful, resonant voice made him a popular choice as a narrator for many films and documentaries. I attribute this feature of his career success to the placement of natal Sun (ruler of the 5th house of theater and performance) in Gemini and the 3rd house, signifying his engaging mind and voice. Freeman also became an executive producer, and voiced several cartoon characters. One of his many culminating career events was being awarded a National Medal of Arts by President Barack Obama in September 2016, with transiting Pluto in his 10th house, Saturn opposite natal Sun and conjunct the north node, and transiting Neptune in Pisces again squaring natal Sun.

Several additional details resonate to the symbolism of his Sun semi-square Pluto in Cancer in the 4th house, which can represent some kind of complicated circumstances in the family heritage. In 2008, Freeman discovered that his Caucasian maternal great-great grandfather had lived with, and was buried beside Freeman's African-American great-great-grandmother; the two could not legally marry in the segregated South. Pluto in the 4th house can be considered a symbol of this crucial family secret. The 4th house also governs our genealogy and ethnic heritage. Later in his life, Freeman discovered through DNA tests that he's descended in part from the Songhai and Tuareg peoples of Nigeria.

Finally, with Venus rising, dispositing the 2nd house and two planets in Taurus, sextile the Aquarius Moon in the 11th house, Freeman has a strong political consciousness and is a noted philanthropist who donates extensively to charitable causes, thus expressing what Holland calls a *social* vocational interest.

Those with *social* interests enjoy relating, supporting, guiding, counseling, and teaching others. The social work environment encourages people to be understanding of each other, to work with others, helping them with personal or career problems, teaching, affecting others spiritually, and being socially responsible. Those with social interests emphasize values such as idealism, kindness, friendliness, generosity, and often work in education, social service, mental health professions, teaching, marriage counseling, clinical psychology, speech pathology, psychiatry. The social personality type has an interest in helping people through teaching, counseling, or private personal services such as astrological counseling. They enjoy solving problems through discussion and teamwork.

Aspects of Venus to most planets (especially Sun, Moon, Mercury, Mars, Jupiter, Uranus and Neptune), and especially Sun-Venus aspects (conjunction or semisquare) can signify an affable, affectionate person who enjoys social interaction. Social vocational interests also reflect the influences of Moon and Jupiter. Angular placement of the Moon, aspects of Sun-Moon, Moon-Venus, and Moon-Jupiter generally show an emotionally attuned, sensitive, caring person with interests in guiding and counseling others, being supportive and nurturing, sometimes through cooking or caregiving roles. Moon-Saturn aspects can represent being emotionally responsible to someone, even when it isn't fun.

Deborah, a massage therapist, has an exact sesquiquadrate of Moon-Venus. With three planets in Virgo she knows her anatomy and bodywork technique very well, but the essence of her success in this work is the way she supports people emotionally.

Cameron, a Jungian analyst, born just before a Full Moon, with Moon in Cancer, is a therapist who listens empathically to people's problems. With Venus opposite Mars near the Ascendant/Descendant, he has strong social vitality and genuinely likes people.

Aidan, mother of three children, is a clinical social worker who helps children with various disadvantages. Moon is her most elevated planet and forms a grand trine with Pluto in Virgo and Sun-Mercury-Venus in Capricorn in the 5th house of children and youth services. Moon trine Sun-Venus symbolizes her social vocational interests, as her work involves counseling, nurturing, and emotionally supporting others.

The social type may also be strongly influenced by Neptune, planet of selfless works. Those with prominent Neptune can be altruistic and devoted to service. An intensive care nurse named Tina has Sun-Neptune in Scorpio in her 5th house, and Mars in Pisces at the MC. Her life is balanced between devotion to her patients (Pisces: hospitals) and to her daughter, as well as daily meditation.

Career counselors use the Holland model to identify a person's strengths, to offer a portrait of their primary vocational type. The way I like to use the theory is to strive to develop in all six areas of our vocational life. By developing competency in many of these vocational interest areas, we have the greatest chance of success and fulfillment in work. While one or more of the interest areas is inevitably less developed, we can still strive for well-rounded development, combining types—for example, becoming an enterprising artistic type.

Mike has owned his own plant nursery and horticultural center for many years and has about a dozen employees. With Sun in the 11th house, he has created a community hub where people congregate to shop and attend classes and lectures addressing social issues pertaining to gardening and land usage. He works to promote sustainability in agriculture and horticulture. He doesn't make a large profit; during the winter months it's often difficult to pay the bills. But he endures (Sun widely conjunct Saturn). Mike is an example of someone achieving fulfillment through a career engaging all six vocational interests and aptitudes: *enterprising*, as it involves sales, entrepreneurship; *conventional*: following procedures, watering schedules, bookkeeping and accounting; *realistic*: construction, building greenhouses, repairs and upkeep, servicing machinery; *social*: his business requires skill in social interaction, welcoming people, talking to customers; and offering workshops, teaching and consulting. He employs *investigative* abilities in constantly researching tree, plant, and flower varieties; and also, through writing, journalism, publishing newspaper columns and newsletters. With Mercury conjunct Saturn and Pluto, Mike is a wealth of information; he's sparse with his words, but when he speaks people listen; and *artistic* interests are expressed in how his nursery is beautifully

Deborah
Natal Chart
August 8, 1963
Tropical   Porphyry   Mean Node

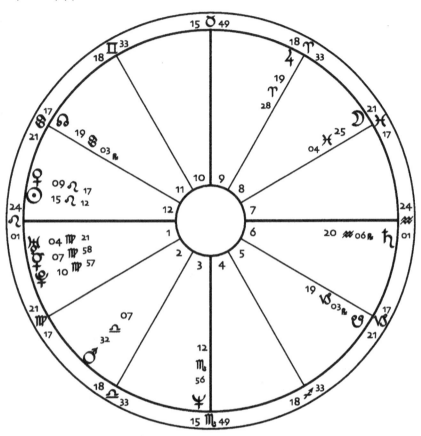

designed, plus they host big seasonal garden parties with food, music, jugglers, sculpture, and body art. Mike is also an excellent musician.

During a lengthy progressed Sun square Saturn, Mike has been struggling to keep his business afloat through tireless hard work and self-discipline. His progressed Sun is also approaching conjunction with progressed Jupiter. There are financial adversities but there's reason for him to be hopeful for ultimate success in his enterprise. However, there's an immediate crisis to deal with. Recently Mike had tran-

Cameron
Natal Chart
January 24, 1948
Tropical   Porphyry   Mean Node

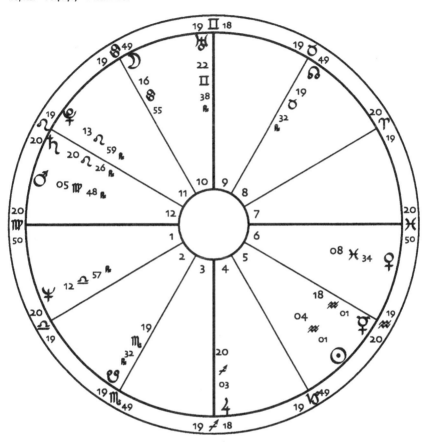

siting Pluto square his Ascendant and he suddenly faced a mutiny of several employees who turned against him and brought up various grievances about his management style, his impatience and brusqueness. These challenges became more meaningful when viewed through an astrological lens. It still hurts, but now at least the pain means something. In the end, he said, it was good that some long-time employees left and new blood entered the business. With transiting Pluto square the Libra Ascendant, several people he used to be close to will no lon-

Aidan
Natal Chart
January 16, 1970
Tropical   Porphyry   Mean Node

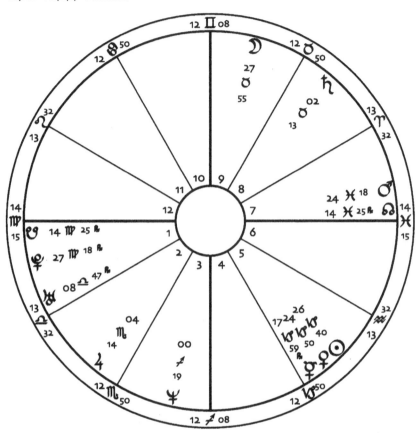

ger speak to him. Some personal imperfections got exposed; that often happens when Pluto brings challenges to the ego and insults to the self. But breaking off relationships involves both parties; we may bear some responsibility, but other people have their own problems to work out too. When Pluto visits, it's time to prune away dead branches, to clean out the closets and cupboards, to let go of what's no longer alive. We can set ourselves in a determined state of mind where that's okay. We can live with it and go on, knowing that we possess innate strength, and feeling renewed intensity about our goals and life purpose.

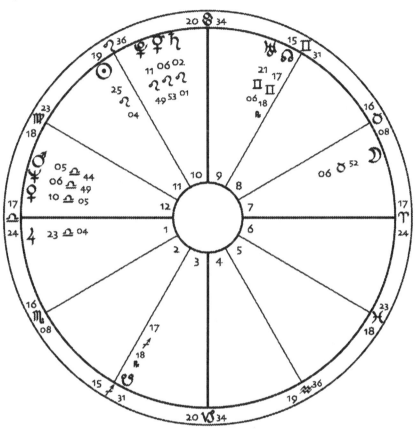

From an astrological perspective there are several other vocational interest areas not mentioned by Holland; for example, Jupiter, Sagittarius, or 9th house emphasis signifies what I'd term philosophical, theological, priestly, or spiritual vocational interests. I don't think these should be considered mere variants or subcategories of investigative interests because these are specifically concerned with a search for truth, knowledge, and meaning; think of someone like Ellen, the Episcopal priest. Another example of this propensity for spirituality is found in Gershom Scholem, the renowned scholar of Jewish mysticism, who had

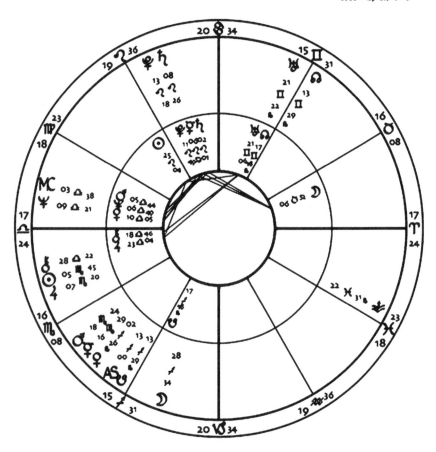

Jupiter rising, Sun, Mercury, Mars, Saturn, and Uranus in Sagittarius, opposing Neptune and Pluto in Gemini (sign of languages and textual translation) at the MC. When somebody's chart emphasizes Mars, we can distinguish a somatic vocational interest related to individual and team sports, hatha yoga, martial arts, dance or other systems of self-culture through trained physical exertion, movement, and competition. I also think there could be a separate Virgo category for health and nutrition interests, and a vocational category for political, social,

activist interests, associated with Uranus and Aquarius. Ralph Nader
has Sun-Mars in Pisces, opposite Neptune, symbol of a selfless servant
of humanity. Saturn is conjunct his north node in Aquarius, representing his decades of work for consumer safety and social and environmental responsibility.

Then there are people drawn to Plutonic vocational pursuits
including shamanic and healing arts—which aren't included in Hol-

Gershom Scholem
Natal Chart
December 5, 1897
12:15:00 AM CET
Berlin, Germany
52N30 / 13E22
Tropical   Koch   Mean Node

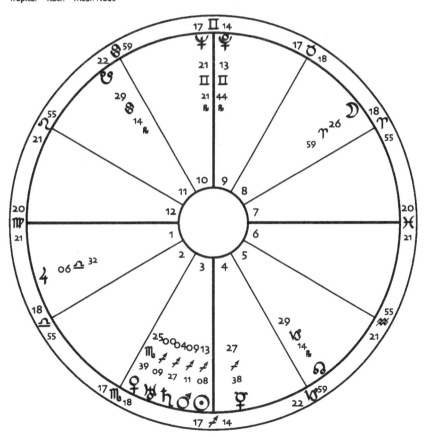

land's typology. Dr. Elisabeth Kubler-Ross, whose revolutionary work transformed societal attitudes about death and dying, had Sun conjunct Pluto in Cancer, trine Saturn in Scorpio in the 8th house. The hospice movement owes its origin to her work. Roshi Joan Halifax has Sun conjunct Mercury and Pluto; after a career as an anthropologist she became a teacher of socially engaged spirituality whose work emphasizes compassionate care for the dying (Sun-Pluto). Their birth charts can be found in *Astrology and Spiritual Awakening*.

Allie has Saturn in the 2nd house in Virgo, conjunct the South node. She does hard physical labor cleaning houses and working in an organic garden. Her work includes construction, building water ponds and gardens. These realistic vocational interests and capacities balance her out and provide financial sustenance for her spiritual work as a trance medium—indicated by a wide Sun-Neptune conjunction and Pisces Moon near the north node. Her natal Sun is sandwiched between Saturn and Neptune showing the need to integrate pragmatism and mysticism, aligning the vibrational influences of material and spiritual worlds. In addition to having Pluto at the Ascendant, her north node is in Pisces in the 8th house, which governs all experiences of interpenetration of boundaries, ranging from sex to interpersonal financial agreements and commitments, to serving as a trance channel for psychic entities.

Vocational astrology further expands career counseling by validating spirituality as a life pursuit. For some people with prominent placement or aspects of Neptune or planets in Pisces, the highest calling in life is to achieve enlightenment. The Tibetan Buddhist teacher, Chogyam Trungpa Rinpoche, embodied the refined intellectual and spiritual clarity and spaciousness of Sun-Mercury-Jupiter in Pisces, opposing Neptune in Virgo. Sun-Jupiter in Pisces represents him as teacher, preceptor, guru, an ocean of wisdom. Sun conjunct Mercury and Jupiter represents intelligence and erudition. Pisces represents what Buddhism calls *bodhi*—enlightenment, the "awakened" state. Trungpa calls this *basic goodness*, "the sanity we're born with." Pisces also represents the truths of egolessness, emptiness, and interconnectedness, and the awakening of great compassion and friendliness (*maitri*).

Ralph Nader

Natal Chart
February 27, 1934
4:52:00 AM EST
Winsted, Connecticut
41N55 / 73W04
Tropical   Porphyry   Mean Node

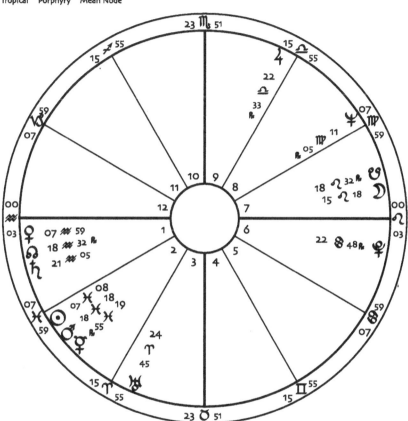

Sun-Jupiter also represents Trungpa Rinpoche's regal demeanor and love of courtly formality and equestrian pursuits. With Uranus sextile his Sun-Jupiter and conjunct Moon's south node, Trungpa was an iconoclastic, free, and individuated personality.

Astrology validates the pursuit of vocational paths that exist outside the traditional Holland vocational model. The Uranian, promethean archetype spurs us to create nontraditional identities, to form our own archetype and boldly actualize it. People such as Jimi Hendrix and

Allie
Natal Chart
September 24, 1950
Tropical   Porphyry   Mean Node

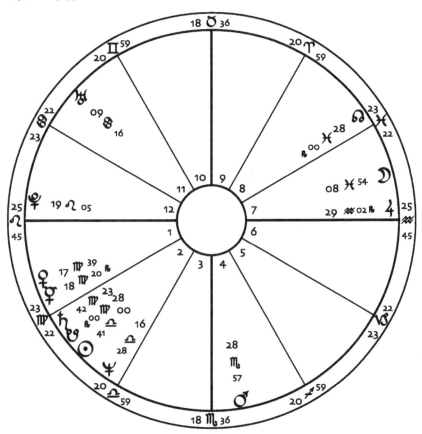

Steve Jobs invented their own archetype and were unlike any other person. Astrology teaches us the self-invention of occupational roles and identities.

Inventor, futurist, outer space explorer, Tesla Motors founder, and visionary entrepreneur Elon Musk (birth time unknown, noon chart) has Sun-Mercury in Cancer square Uranus in Libra. Moon in Virgo. The Sun-Uranus square symbolizes his unique ventures in practical scientific inquiry at the cutting edge of technological innovation. With a Saturn-

Chogyam Trungpa

Natal Chart
February 28, 1939
5:23:00 AM LMT
Llasa, Tibet
29N39 / 91E10
Tropical Porphyry Mean Node

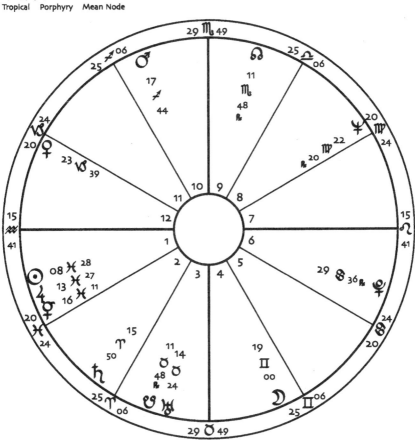

Neptune opposition, he's someone who has made a vision come true.

The value of astrology for vocational counseling is that our chart symbolism allows each of us to envision our potentials and faithfully work to realize them. In so doing, we achieve the embodiment and expression of spiritual, archetypal essences that expand the meaning of each facet and each gesture of life.

Elon Musk
Natal Chart
June 28, 1971
12:00:00 PM 2E
Pretoria, South Africa
25S45 / 28E10
Tropical   Porphyry   Mean Node

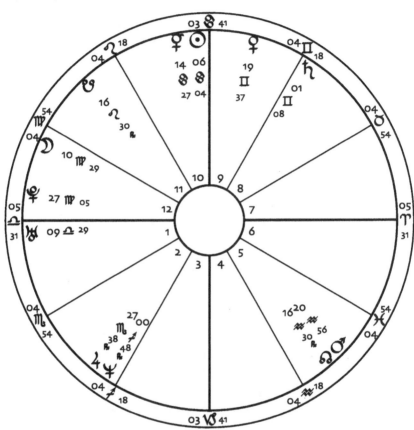

CHAPTER 6

Sound of the Cosmos:
Astrology and Music in the Evolution
of Consciousness

Thus far I've addressed how I utilize astrology in several realms: as a tool for emotional healing in psychotherapy; as a means for identifying and consciously participating in archetypal patterns of transformation synchronously expressed in dream symbols; as a guide to efficiency and productivity in daily life; and as a clarifying lens for focused career and occupational guidance. I've spoken of the practical benefits of astrology and the special importance of the Saturn cycle.[47] But now I want to go in a different direction, because things are changing for me.

This chapter has been written during my progressed balsamic Moon phase, a period of internal closure, endings, and completion of a long 30-year cycle. A whole new cycle is about to begin in my life as I approach a progressed New Moon in Pisces, with Sun and Moon in exact semisquare to natal and progressed Venus. The semisquare is a neglected aspect in astrology, but it's just as potent as a square or an opposition. This progressed New Moon-semisquare-Venus represents the fact that my path is increasingly through music. Playing music has always been one of my favorite activities, starting when I took my first guitar lessons at age 11. When I was 15, I had a progressed Full Moon with progressed Sun conjunct natal and progressed Venus. I played classical guitar recitals and learned rock, blues, jazz, and folk music. After college I was a traveling street musician and played a few humble gigs in restaurants and clubs. I continued playing and songwriting through my Saturn return. At my Uranus opposition I started playing out a bit in clubs and studying jazz intensively. I'm not saying I was very good but I put myself out there for the fun of it, to satisfy my natal Uranus in Leo opposite Venus. The urge to study and play and compose music has always been strongest for me at times of transits and progressions involving Venus. With this progressed New Moon, I'm drawing in a new in-breath, beginning something completely different. Thus, this chapter carries the feeling of my progressed balsamic phase and progressed New Moon and marks the beginning of a new cycle in my own evolution.

Astrology aids our intelligent movement through time, in the world of work and human relations, but it's also about mysteries, beauty, and subtle, vibrational matters that I intuit have something to do with the music of the cosmos. Recently my thinking about this was stirred by witnessing demonstrations of the creative power of sound based on research in the field of *cymatics*, the study of vibrational phenomena. The term was coined by Hans Jenny, a Swiss Anthroposophist. In cymatics, the surface of a plate or membrane is vibrated and regions of displacement are made visible in a thin coating of particles, paste, or liquid. Different patterns emerge in the excitatory medium depending on the geometry of the plate and the driving frequency; the patterns of lines are called nodal lines of the vibration mode. It occurs to me in this moment that planetary influences have a similar formative vibrational effect that makes visible our own internal geometry and can help us to gradually actualize it.

Those who are well attuned to their natal structure and adopt it as a template for growth begin to sound a distinctive tone in the universe, as the personality refined and unified by astrology evolves into a great song. Earlier I discussed how I practice astrology combined with dreams, and in concert with the goals and methods of psychotherapy. Now I want to contemplate some higher octaves of astrology and share some speculations on the astrology of music and the music of astrology. How can these two catalysts of consciousness join forces?

I believe music and astrology are practices that can coevolve and influence each other, and that there's a tremendous synergy between them. Music and astrology are brilliant expressions of the human creation of harmony, coherence, and meaning in existence, and are two of the most intelligent means of evoking expansive spiritual states. As evolving beings guided by astrology, we are the composer and the composition. In this chapter we'll examine astrology in relation to principles of rhythm, syncopation, tone, harmony, dissonance, counterpoint, modulation, and form and improvisation in chart interpretation. After some brief historical background, we'll look at some relevant charts, mostly of musicians.

Back in 1984, I received a letter from Dane Rudhyar where he wrote: "Being 'in' the world but not 'of' it is very difficult. It is man's supreme power that he can live consistently at more than one or two levels. Polyphonic, counterpunctual living—Caesar *and* God (say the Gospels)." In other words, live a spiritual life, be an astrologer, yogi, meditator, and mystic, but also show up to work, pay your taxes, honor Saturn, be in the world. This was the origin of my thinking of astrology as musical.

Ancient writers Plato, Cicero, Plutarch described the sounds and harmony of celestial spheres, a harmony corresponding to the evenness of planetary motions. The philosopher Plotinus wrote, "All music, based upon melody and rhythm, is the earthly representative of heavenly music."[48] Later, Johannes Kepler wrote, "[W]e should not be surprised that men discovered the beautiful, effective succession of tones in the musical modes when we see that in so doing they did nothing but imitate God's work, thereby playing down to earth the drama of the celestial motions."[49]

According to Joscelyn Godwin, in the ancient *Corpus Hermeticum*, Hermes Trismegistus describes:

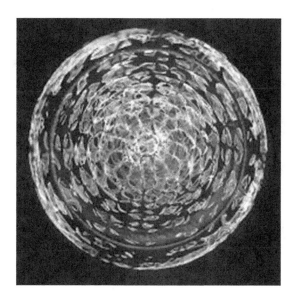

the image of the Soul ascending through the planetary spheres and hearing the planetary music on the way. . . . The Hermetic voyager transcends the planetary harmony—the realm where the Soul is made—to rise in his purified being to the harmony of the invisible world, whereupon another ladder of ascent leads eventually to his deification. Elsewhere the treatise Poimandres also describes the descent of the Soul, which takes on the psychological qualities of each planet . . . as it passes down through the spheres. It is these qualities or energies that are summarized in the natal horoscope. . . . Each incarnate being therefore sounds . . . a different chord of the planetary or psychological harmonies, and it is this that causes *musica humana* (the music of the human being) to resemble *musica mundana* (the music of the worlds or spheres).[50]

The gnostic teachings stated that at the moment of death the soul would once again rise up through the spheres, shedding attachment and identification with the character of each planet and return to a pure state in the Pleroma of divine luminosity. The same thing can be achieved through mystical practices and purification, including spiritual astrology.

Marsilio Ficino, instigator of the Italian Renaissance, linked astrology and music, writing:

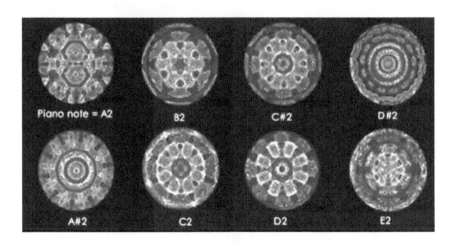

tones first chosen by the rule of the stars and then combined according to the contiguity of these stars with each other make a sort of common form [presumably a melody or chord] and in it a celestial power arises. It is indeed very difficult to judge exactly what kinds of tones are suitable for what sorts of stars, which combination of tones especially accord with what sorts of constellations and aspects. But we can attain this, partly through our own efforts, partly by some divine destiny . . . [, through] inspired prophecy. [51]

That's where our work as astrologers begins. What is the tone or music that's called forth by our planets and stars? By consciously developing the psychological and archetypal qualities of each planet we evolve an individuated personality, sounding a distinctive chord.

In his book *The World is Sound: Music and the Landscape of Consciousness,* Joachim-Ernst Berendt wrote:

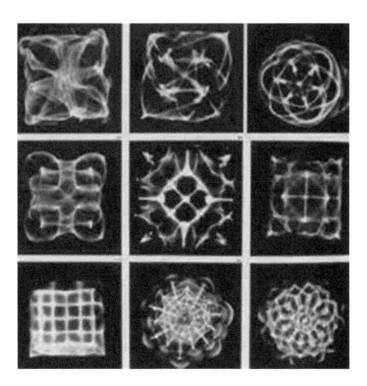

The most famous work of Johannes Kepler was entitled "Five Books About World Harmony," as if it were music he had written about rather than planets. . . . Pythagoras and Ptolemy both anticipated correlations between the orbit of the planets and the vibrations of a taut string. . . . [Kepler noted] how precise the harmonical structure of our solar system is. According to Kepler, God was master of the cosmic sounds, causing the planets to leave their inherently circular orbits and to adopt the conspicuously complicated elliptical orbit in order to produce even more beautiful sounds. . . . [52]

Berendt cites the Swiss philosopher Hans Kayser, who wrote:

The concept of the harmony of the spheres is as old as the first awakening of mankind to consciousness. First in myth, then in astral symbolism, . . . this concept became the presupposition for astrology and the first astronomical inquiries of all ancient peoples. Kepler however was the first who gave it that foundation which lifts it out of mere faith and brings it in line with modern scientific thinking. In his main work, the *Harmonia Mundi*, . . . he shows . . . that between the mutual velocities of the planets there exists a great number of musical harmonies. . . . [F]or anyone who has read the works of Kepler and allowed his enthusiasm to transport him, Kepler's harmonic proportions are spiritual realities. He knows that here we are not dealing with mere formulations . . . but with the truly shattering experience of *Tat twam asi*: This is you. There are powers above and shapes written in the sky which sound in your own soul, which concern you most vitally, and which belong to the Godhead as much as to you in your innermost self. [53]

Through aligning our individual consciousness and entire life purpose with planetary motions, we achieve union with the harmony of the spheres. This is the spiritual mystery at the heart of our discipline. Berendt continues:

Of particular interest is the fact that as the orbits of the planets change (as they do constantly), the angular velocities relative to the sun at the so-called aphelia and perihelia (the two extreme points of the elliptical orbits of the planets) remain

Marsilio Ficino, from a fresco painted by Domenico Ghirlandalo, Tornabuoni Chapel, Santa Maria; Bust of Marsilio Ficino by Andrea Ferruccini, Florence's Cathedral

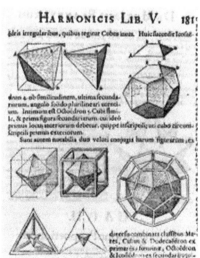

Portrait of Johannes Kepler, unknown artist, 1610; Illustration from Kepler, Harmonia Mundi

nearly constant. These angular velocities are the basis for computing harmonic proportions. . . . [P]oets again and again over the centuries have sensed an "inner harmony" while looking at the starry sky. . . . [T]his "inner harmony" is really our own sound . . . inasmuch as all the "aspects" arrived at by way of harmonics and mathematics are also astrological aspects. . . . [T]he elements of classical astrology of course can also be understood harmonically. It is obvious that a conjunction is an octave, an opposition is a fifth, a trigon [trine] a fourth, a quintile a minor third, a biquintile a minor sixth, etc. In the final analysis then, the horoscope of a person (or of an event) is a system of chords and sounds. *Man "sounds."* [54]

In this chapter we contemplate how it is that man and woman sound. It's also worth noting that modern astronomy confirms that we live in a universe of sound. Berendt wrote:

[Modern scientists have measured the] low humming of the Cancer pulsar . . . emitting pulses . . . with breaks of ten or twenty seconds between each one. . . . [In space] there is ticking and drumming, humming and crackling. . . . Space is filled with sound. . . . [Planets such as Jupiter emit sounds, as does the sun, which hisses and makes crackling sounds or] roars of alarming intensity. . . . The most interesting producers of sound in space are the pulsars, . . . pulsating stars or neutron stars [—very small, very high density]. . . . Pulsating stars . . . possess unimaginably strong magnetic fields, and they are constantly encircled by fierce electrical storms. Some pulsars sound like bongo drums, others like castanets, still others like the scratching needle of a record player. . . . The cosmos is filled with sounds and rhythms, from pulsars and quasars, from supernovas, from so-called "red giants" and "white dwarfs," from fleeting and colliding star systems, and, course, from our own sun. [55]

If we're surrounded by sound, it must be inscribed in our cells, in our bodies, as the formative principle of life; the research in the field

Sun

Hubble telescope image of Jupiter

Pulsating star

Crab pulsar, a neutron star about
28–30 km across, at the center of the
Crab Nebula.

of cymatics demonstrates that sound has an internal geometry that shapes creation. The connection between tone and the geometry of life goes to the heart of how reality is organized. And if planets send out tones, how do they organize our reality? Our task as astrologers is to tune in and perceive the sounds and music of the cosmos, to sense the tonality and rhythms woven into every strand of creation and every moment of time, as we come to perceive this through attunement to the planets.

So, cognizant of the music of the spheres, let's return to our theme. Another starting point for my reflections is the illustration of the alchemist Basil Valentine with symbols of planets and musical notes and

The Alchemist Basil Valentine [56]

instruments appearing together, hinting that astrology and music are related disciplines in the process of self-transformation.

That's the idea I'm pursuing here. Of course, in ancient India all the sacred sciences were inter-related—jyotisha, ayurveda, yoga, and music. Astrology is a transformative yoga, a unifying discipline, as is music for those who study and involve themselves with it seriously. Both astrology and music are paths of self-development and self-expression. They are both yogas, paths of self-unification, insofar as these disciplines require attention, presence, concentration, overcoming fear, sounding a clear tone, and becoming refined in one's personal demeanor and self-expression. Music and astrology have the power to awaken us to states of consciousness outside the mundane, the profane, to tap our sense of the sacred, our perception of a greater beauty and harmony. Both can transform our embodiment. Music affects you vibrationally. Your body feels different. It wants to move and dance or be still in response to music. And as astrologers we resonate to the various planets so that we act, feel, and think differently. Music and astrology both connect us to a wider universe of feeling and consciousness; they evoke awe, enrich everyday life, put a bounce in our step, a smile on our face, tears in our eyes. Two of the primordial human activities, they're fun, uplifting, and make life bearable.

Both astrology and music help us establish a state of consciousness or deliberately change it. We create our environment and its ambience through sound and can modify or enhance our state of consciousness by choosing to compose, play, or listen to music that matches what is going on astrologically. We can get ourselves going and raise our energy with rock and roll. We can calm ourselves or ease into sleep with healing sounds, chill with space music or electronica. We can propel ourselves into trance and visionary states with drumming, toning, songs of devotion and ecstasy; have an emotional catharsis with emo rock or heavy metal; feed our romantic excitement or longing with love songs; create holiday cheer with Christmas music or other festive sounds; create a sacred atmosphere conducive to meditation with Gregorian chant or Hindu devotional chanting. And we can commiserate with ourselves during times of suffering by listening to the blues.

Astrologically we change our state of consciousness by looking at this present moment in terms of the planetary forces acting upon us and within us. When Moon is conjunct Neptune or when transiting Neptune rises, sets, or culminates, I like to set myself into a relaxed frame of mind, preferably under a tree or in a bathtub, meditating quietly, or resting on a bed or couch. I invite and make space for that experience. And I can set myself in a work frame of mind during major transits involving Saturn or at the daily rising, culminating, or setting of Saturn. When Venus is accentuated, we put our touch of beauty and artistry on some facet of our life, and we can change our state of consciousness by putting on fresh clothes, and becoming enthused about social life and going out into the world to connect with other people. And there are moments like the present time, as I write this, during a Sun-Mercury-Neptune conjunction in Pisces, a time to change my state of consciousness by setting aside time from the cares and business of life to meditate and reflect on mysticism and mysteries and how our work as astrologers is connected to an ancient and still-living gnosis. I explain this point in the Inset Text (see pages 176–177).

My awareness of the gnostic nature of astrology has been influenced by the ideas of mystic scholar Antoine Faivre. According to Faivre, astrology in the West emerged as a branch within the tradition of esotericism, the study of secret, hidden, mystical knowledge, knowledge that brings about an experience of initiation and transmutation of being.[57] For centuries, esotericism—encompassing the teachings of astrology, alchemy, and magic—has been a counterpart to our scientific, secularized vision of the world, offering instead an advanced form of mythic-imaginal thought. Esotericism seeks to explain the interior meaning of symbols, myth, and reality, through elucidation and interpretation, known as hermeneutics. Astrology is interpretation of the sky—celestial hermeneutics. Astrologers read the text of a birth chart or current transiting formation and align with it, reinterpreting past or current events, transforming our life situations by bathing them in the light of archetypal meanings.

Faivre calls esotericism "an ensemble of forms of spirituality,"[58] focused on the principles of correspondences, living nature, imagination, and transmutation. The doctrine of correspondences posits symbolic or energetic correspondences between all parts of the universe, microcosm and macrocosm. These correspondences are ordinarily veiled and must be read or decoded. Faivre writes, "The entire universe is . . . a set of hieroglyphs to decipher; everything is a sign, everything harbors and manifests mystery."[59] As astrologers we study correspondences between the celestial realm and the material world, between planets and the human body, believing that we're part of everything and that the surrounding cosmos is also inside us. According to Faivre, esotericism views nature as a living entity pervaded by a divine presence or life-force. Nature "is seen, known, and felt to be essentially alive in all its parts."[60] Thus, it's believed that various "magical" means can be utilized to redeem and regenerate nature and to reestablish harmony and wholeness, such as the use of gemstones, metals, ritual acts, dance, but also chanting, music, mantric tone vibration, and acts of creative imagination. This insight leads us to our present consideration of correspondences between planetary energies and musical tones, rhythm, and harmony.

In the esoteric arts, mediating symbols enable us to gain access to the sacred, to spiritual knowledge, through the practice of creative imagination. Symbols connect the divine spiritual world and Nature. Astrologers approach the planets as mediators of an imaginal world that facilitates harmony between the world of spiritual archetypes and our human embodiment in nature. Planetary symbols are representations of a particular moment or facet of consciousness and can also induce a higher level of organization within the personality. Astrologers build structures of consciousness through contemplating a celestial formation (such as the Uranus-Pluto square or a Saturn-Pluto conjunction) and acting in accord with it, in vibrational resonance with the whole, even during chaotic, cacophonous moments within the collective sphere.

In esotericism the use of imagination is based on the Corpus Hermeticum, the ancient teaching of Hermes Trismegistus (rediscovered at the end of the fifteenth century), especially the statement "as above, so below," the idea that the microcosm includes the macrocosm; thus it's efficacious to practice the imaginal interiorization of the world within our mind. Faivre writes, "Thus understood, imagination . . . is a tool for knowledge of the self, of the world, of myth. It is the eye of fire penetrating the surface of appearances, in order to make meanings, connections, burst forth, to render the invisible visible."[61] Astrologers scan with the eye of fire to perceive how each moment is organized, rooted in the awareness that we're a part of everything, including the planets and the creative tensions between them. We can even imagine that the entire planetary drama is, in some sense, unfolding inside of us. This helps us align with even the most complex circuitry of celestial energies and stay on course while the social and environmental changes on our planet are accelerating.

In the spiritual practices of esoteric schools, the goal is an experience of transmutation, a term that indicates that something passes from one level to another and that the elements constituting it are modified. "Transmutation," a term borrowed from alchemy, is "metamorphosis." Lead becomes silver, silver becomes gold. Responding to the energies and messages of each moment can change our substance, our embodiment, so that we continually change form and keep going to other levels.

Astrology and Tone-Magic: Structure and Improvisation

Like astrology, there are no limits to music, no limits to what you can do with it, or how far you can go with it. Music is conscious intonation through our voices, our hands, our instruments. In his book, *The Magic of Tone and the Art of Music*, Rudhyar wrote that music in ancient cultures was "*tone-magic* . . . [utilizing] sound as a power of communication and creation]."[62]

> Metaphysically, Sound refers to the release of a power that . . . precipitates the divine idea into material, objective manifestation. . . . [S]ound should be understood as the power of the divine will, which sets in motion the proto-matter of chaos. . . . This creative Sound makes matter spin into vortices of motion. . . . [Rudhyar notes] the capacity of music to arouse feelings which induce emotions . . . [and] the power of sound to heal and reinvigorate an organism. . . . Tone . . . is almost synonymous with potency. A state of tension is also implied, as a violin string needs to be stretched and tensed in order to produce tones. Whatever is too relaxed lacks tone. . . . The universe is the product of a creative release of power. . . . In terms of pure energy, this creative release is sound. . . . A tone is a sound that . . . convey[s] significant information to the consciousness of the hearer. . . . Thus a tone is a meaning-carrying sound. [63]

Astrology gets our identities clarified and focused so we have tone—lean, cohesive form, and potency, and develop the optimal level of tension and arousal, poised to unfold ourselves with energy. Fully living one's chart and one's destiny is a practice of tone magic. That's what astrology is for—to help us become resonant instruments for the song, the music that wants to come through us. Our identity is inscribed in our nativities. It's like we're handed a piece of sheet music by the creator and told, now play this, play this part in the cosmic symphony. The birth chart is like the score for the song or composition of your life—how it could sound, how it could be arranged and orchestrated. And just as musicians breathe life into the written note or score, astrologers

Rudhyar composing at his piano [64]

need to breathe life into planetary symbols and bring the chart and the planets alive, and thus to make our lives into music. Rudhyar observed that musical notes can be depotentialized by being set down in writing as abstract notes and need to have their spiritual potency activated.[65] It's the same thing with using our will and imagination to develop our planets in astrology. You become familiar with the tones of each planet so when your next Mars transit comes around you activate your Mars; you know what to do. We use our foreknowledge of planetary transits to form anticipations, more than to predict specific occurrences.

Rudhyar's book begins with the idea that music is an expression of "man's primary need: communication." It is communication and expression, not random noise, such as the sound of the refrigerator or traffic roar. Music is deliberate sound expression and communication combining tone, rhythm, melody, harmony. Expressing one's chart consciously is also a conscious communication and emanation of who we are. A birth isn't random. It's intentional, a potential response to a social or collective need. That's the creed of humanistic astrologers. Through the birth chart the universe communicates the purpose of the individual's birth. And awakening to ourselves through astrology we're able to define and announce that purpose and sound it forth.

In its inception, music is discovered—spontaneous and unexpected. Music is also repeated, practiced, refined, or recalled in memory; so it becomes set, organized. Music is thus deliberate and intentional. The practice of astrology also involves both spontaneity and organization. The spontaneity comes through discovering the meaning of chart symbols in quiet moments of contemplation. Rudhyar wrote:

> The astrological chart is . . . not something merely to be studied with a coldly analytical intellect. It is something to be *felt*. . . . Face the chart as an artist faces a painting, in positive and keenly aware openness to it, with the eager determination to *evoke* the significance of it. . . . Face the chart . . . in an attitude of "prayer," asking for inner guidance and the bestowal of wise understanding.[66]

An astrologer's open awareness invites new, unexpected, and revelatory insights. Over time, with practice and years of study, the interpretation of one's birth chart and transits grows refined and precise, just as a musician confidently performs a well-practiced song or composition. Both music and chart interpretation adhere to principles of form and improvisation. In both disciplines there's value in some unstructured exploration and spontaneous discovery, but many people prefer to follow a structured process, instead of playing music or interpreting a chart randomly and formlessly. It's pleasurable to work out musical parts and arrangements, melodies and chord changes, and to play known songs or compositions, modes or scales. Similarly, most seasoned astrologers read charts according to a procedure, some orderly process of relating to the chart symbolism and bringing it to life. Rudhyar's book, *The Practice of Astrology as a Technique of Human Understanding*[67] describes a series of steps: to understand the nature and purpose of what one is about to study, to assume personal responsibility for the use of our knowledge, to establish a clear procedure of work, and a clear understanding of the meaning of zodiacal signs and houses, the lights, and the planetary system as a whole; acquiring a sense of form and accentuation in the natal chart, forming a dynamic understanding of planetary cycles and aspects, and establishing a proper attitude toward astrological predictions.

There's room in both disciplines for structure and for improvisation. We have to follow some established form and methods. But we don't want to play a piece of music the same way each time. We change how we express and interpret the music, sometimes improvising and playing variations. And it's important not to read charts the same way all the time, and not to read the chart so much through the lens of what other people have said and written. Whenever I speak to clients who know a little astrology, they always repeat the same statements about Mars-Saturn aspects, that this is bad and indicates frustration and "driving with the brakes on." I've heard that so many times. I think it comes from Alan Oken's classic work, *As Above, So Below*. We need a fresh way of relating to symbols such as Mars-Saturn, so it can be realized differently, for example, as focused application of the will, generating force and power. For example, we see strength, power, focus, and determination evident in John Coltrane's Mars-Saturn opposition; he was tremendously self-disciplined as a musician. Rather than just repeating what we've read and staying in interpretive ruts, it's possible to improvise and say something new, bold, and edgy, as long as it's in alignment with the astrological symbolism. That's the main parameter—that we stay within the form and that we don't just make things up. That's part of the astrologer's ethical responsibility: to be true to what the planets indicate.

Jazz is a wonderful form of music to compare with astrology because it combines structure and freedom, form and improvisation. It's the art of improvisation within structure, within the chord changes. This is comparable to improvisation in chart interpretation. The birth chart is like the head or theme in a jazz chart, a statement of the melody and repeating chord changes. Transits are like solos, improvisations, and variations on key themes.

The Trimurti: Brahma, Vishnu, Shiva.   *Shiva Nataraj.*

Silence and the Primal Sound

Several key archetypal moments in astrology correspond to the phenomenon of music. I'm referring to the movement from Pisces silence to Aries cosmic sound. This is comparable to the movement from the 12th house to the Ascendant, and the transition from the balsamic phase of endings and creative silence to New Moon. All refer to the first note that breaks the stillness. Out of silence, a tone. Out of nothingness and stillness emerges a primal tone that conveys the divine will (Aries): Om. There really isn't one astrological symbol that can adequately represent the *mysterium tremendum*, the cosmic power or tone that sets in motion divine manifestation. Insofar as Pluto can be considered the co-ruler of Aries it is signifier of seed rebirth, passages into and out of the world; thus, we could interpret Pluto as a symbol of the power of cosmic vibration, the first tone and the last note, birth and death, the inception of sound and its cessation. Hinduism portrays this as Brahma, Vishnu, and Shiva, primordial reality that creates, sustains, and destroys. In Sanskrit, this is the principle termed *Nada Brahma*.

According to Joachim Berendt:

These two images depict Arhanarishvara, the androgynous Shiva.

Nada Brahma is a Sanskrit word meaning "sound." [It is related to the word *nadi*,] "meaning "river" or "stream" but also "rushing" or "sounding." . . . The term *nadi* is also used to mean "stream of consciousness," a meaning that goes back four thousand years to . . . the *Rig-Veda*. . . . *Nada Brahma* means: Sound is God. . . . Or vice versa: God is Sound. . . . The principle of Brahma, the so-called *Brahman*, is the prime power of the cosmos, the inner consciousness of man and of all living things. . . . So *Nada Brahma* means not only: God, the Creator, is sound; but also: . . . Creation, the cosmos, the world, is sound. And: Sound is the world.[68]

The Hindu dancing god Shiva Nataraj is a symbol of energy in motion, the creative vibration within the divine stillness and omnipresent consciousness. Shiva is androgynous—Ardhanarishvara, a union of male-female, Shiva-Shakti. And one of Shiva's hands holds a drum, signifying the rhythm of time and creation. I also appreciate the wavy bends in Shiva's body, which manifests dynamic energy in motion, the thrilling Shakti that enlivens Shiva's tranquility.

Celestial Rhythms

One thing music and astrology have in common is their focus on time and rhythm. There's no music without rhythm. Whether it's the sound of our mother's heartbeat, the shaman's drum, the pulse of African drums, the percussion of a symphony or a jazz or rock band, rhythm is the origin of music. Music plays with our sense of time; it goes faster, slower, either staccato or legato. Change has rhythm, a forward motion. We catch the beat, flow with the rhythm, flow with the changes. Rhythm is the pulse of music. And rhythm is at the heart of astrology, the study of planetary cycles. It's about time and how we organize it. In the endless expanse of time there are gradations and nuances in the quality of the time moment.

Complex rhythms are at work in the sky and the unfolding of the chart, as we observe lunar returns, solar returns, Mars returns, Jupiter returns, Saturn returns, and so forth. Each planetary cycle follows a different rhythm and, unfolding concurrently, these cycles create poly-rhythms. From a geocentric perspective the Sun transits and returns to its birthplace each year, a kind of annual reset or return to origins that gives a direction to the individual's year, like the return to the top of a song or tune. The Moon's monthly rhythm defines a consistent pulse of life; things are at a lull during a waning Moon; things pick up pace and momentum after New Moon, during the cycle's waxing phases, and reach a crescendo at Full Moon. In waning planetary phases, the music of life winds down, whereas near Full Moon, life reaches an energetic and emotional climax. This is the familiar rhythm of the cyclic process.

There's also the Mercury cycle, with its characteristic rhythm of retrograde cycles and transiting inferior and superior conjunctions with the Sun, marking periods when the tempo of life speeds up as we rethink and reconsider issues and problems and formulate new insights. Each year I map this out—the Sun-Mercury superior conjunctions and the Sun-Mercury-retrograde conjunctions. For me, these are pivotal astrological events of the year. Plotting these periods in natal houses allows me to plan, to place special attention on thinking about those zones of life. I detail this cycle in *Planets in Therapy*.

Most astrologers also follow the two years Mars cycle, which culminates at the Mars retrograde opposition to the Sun, and the phases of the Jupiter cycle, when we make plans and get our hopes up a bit. And there's the steady rhythm of the Saturn cycle, where every 7–8 years we reach a crucial phase of the cycle. Uranus's 84-year cycle can be divided into two 42-year phases, three 28-year phases, four 21-year phases or twelve 7-year phases. This is discussed by Alexander Ruperti in *Cycles of Becoming.*[69] Each planet has its own tempo, its own rhythm and characteristic tone.

I consider not only the temporal duration of planetary cycles but also the vibratory quality of planets. For example, a person whose chart accentuates Mercury, especially in Gemini or Virgo, on an angle, or aspecting the Moon, tends to be wired, quick, busy. The tempo of life for that person can be frenetic. Contrast this with Saturn's tempo, which is slow, steady, predictable.

This is the music of astrology, the process of following the rhythms of various planetary cycles and becoming entrained with them. Multiple voices coordinate. Syncopation, the shifting of a normal accent in musical rhythm, is seen in the way transit cycles intersect, and minor transits punctuate and spice up slower outer planet rhythms and give the music of our lives energy and motion. In addition to outer planet transits, I track the passages of transiting Sun, Moon, Mercury, Venus, and Mars. This is detailed in *Planets in Therapy*. This is also comparable to musical *counterpoint*, where several voices or instruments sound simultaneously, playing off each other. Astrologers attend to all the planets and to multiple realms of life and move through various activities and responsibilities smoothly. Thus, a life shaped and informed by astrology becomes musical, counterpunctual, allowing us to reach levels of integration not easily accessible through other disciplines.

J. S. Bach (Noon Chart), who developed counterpoint, had Aries Sun trine Mars (think of the energy and vitality of his music), and notice the prominence of Venus: Venus conjunct Mercury in Pisces, square Mars in Sagittarius, trine Pluto in Cancer, semisquare Uranus in Taurus; Venus and Mercury oppose Saturn in Virgo, representing flowing musical lines executed with meticulous detail. He was born at the

Full Moon conjunct Jupiter in Libra, which signifies the emotionally expansive, uplifting quality and intensity of his music.

There's also counterpoint in the interplay between one's own chart and the charts of spouses, couples, families, organizations, and work groups. In a relationship you acquire a second chart; you have to vibrate to the other person's chart, understanding how they're organized differently than you are, and going through transits together, in unison. The same thing is true if you have children. You acquire new charts with spouses and family members and coworkers, creating rich, complex compositions. Marriages and families are like orchestras where the different instruments sound together and harmonize and play off each other. Astrology is an amazing tool for understanding one another, giving each other space to have our own experience.[70]

Planets and the Chord of Personality

Planets are comparable to notes that make up the chord of personality. Each planet has a different voice and a different agenda. Personality is like a chord constructed from individual notes arrayed in combinations. The study of astrology begins with learning about different planets in our chart and how they operate, how they want to find expression. What does my Moon in the 2nd house need, or my 11th house Sun, or Uranus in my 7th house? We learn how to play our charts one piece at a time, one voice, one instrument, one planet at a time. Then we combine them together. First one sounds the chart as a series of separate tones, then as a song or symphony. Astrologers who develop themselves in accordance with the natal chart sound rich, chordal tones of personality, and thus become distinctive individuals.

Insofar as the chart represents personality as a multi-tone chord, there's a tonic note: the Sun, representing the key that you're in, the root tone. The natal Sun's sign and house placement and primary aspects indicate the primary key or focus of a person's identity. For example, Sun conjunct Saturn in Virgo is in a different key than Sun-Venus conjunction in Aquarius or Sun-Jupiter in Taurus. Let's say that you have Sun in the 6th house and you have to function within the culture of your workplace. Your circumstances require it. That's a primary key in

J. S. Bach
Natal Chart
March 21, 1685
12:00:00 PM LMT
Eisenach, Germany
50N59 / 10E19
Tropical   Porphyry   Mean Node

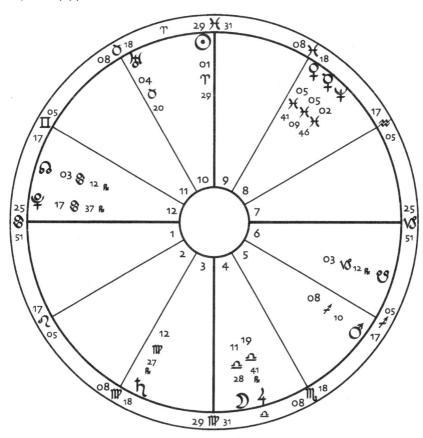

which your life plays out. Or think of Donald Trump's Sun-Uranus conjunction in Gemini. His identity is in its own unique key where provocative communication is central. His Sun sextile Mars-Ascendant in Leo shows his brashness, arrogance, competitiveness, impulsiveness, and addiction to constant self-aggrandizement. The Sun represents the identity that should be fully intonated. If the Sun represents the tonic or root note of the chord, the other planets organize around the Sun and distribute its light, like the notes that build up a chord. Learning to sing or play an instrument requires learning to refine tone and pitch, to hit the note so it's sufficiently in tune, and so too practicing astrology means sounding the tones and chords of our personality, being true to our authentic selves.

Of course, it's possible to place too much importance on ego and individual identity, but I don't think our spiritual path requires that we dismiss or negate this aspect of life in pursuit of a transcendent, egoless state. Since the emergence of a heliocentric worldview in the 16th century, we believe in the spiritual value of orientation to the Sun. The perspective of astrology is that we need to develop solar consciousness, solar identities, while remaining open to the influence of galactic space and its evolutionary pull beyond the ego. Astrology can aid us in ego development and in awakening within archetypal and spiritual dimensions. The ideal is to make yourself a whole unto yourself and within your human relations, and gradually link yourself to a larger whole, larger systems and organizations, and the Being at the center of existence. That's the transpersonal way.[71] The individual personality can henceforth serve as a vessel to convey some portion of divine incandescence. Success in musicianship and in astrology in large part stems from living and emanating the ray of one's solar identity, with graceful self-confidence. Inhabiting and expressing the natal Sun implies being comfortable with oneself and having self-respect, not in an arrogant or self-cherishing way, not with inflated self-importance, but with warmth and a feeling of pride and dignity in the self. Sun brings poise in being oneself, and sounding a clear tone.

If Sun is the root tone of the personality chord, Venus enhances and refines its expression, clothing it in aesthetically satisfying melodies, harmonies, and arrangements. Venus rules music as she represents pleasing form, pleasing sounds. Venus is hugely important in the charts of musicians. The urge to learn music and play music is linked to transits to natal Venus, especially if there's innate interest shown by strong natal Venus placement.

I find that musical talent is indicated by placement of Venus near the angles or in prominent aspects to other planets (especially Sun) or the Moon's nodes. Miles Davis had Venus in Aries sextile Jupiter

Miles Davis
Natal Chart
May 29, 1926
5:00:00 AM CST
Alton, Illinois
38N53 / 90W11
Tropical   Porphyry   Mean Node

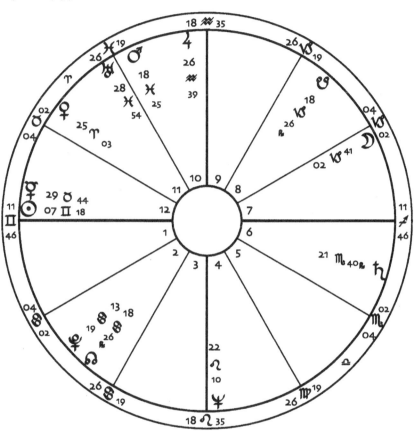

in Aquarius, trine Neptune in Leo, square the nodal axis, and quincunx Saturn in Scorpio. Joan Baez has Venus conjunct the MC, square Neptune. I noted earlier that Taylor Swift has Venus in the 1st house, exactly square the MC and widely conjunct the lunar node. Bonnie Raitt has Venus trine Mars, opposite Uranus, semi-square the Sun, trine her Ascendant, and widely square the lunar nodes. John Coltrane had Venus, dispositor of the Libra Sun, at home in the 7th house and widely

Bonnie Raitt
Natal Chart
November 8, 1949
4:08:00 PM PST
Burbank Junction, California
34N11 / 118W19
Tropical   Porphyry   Mean Node

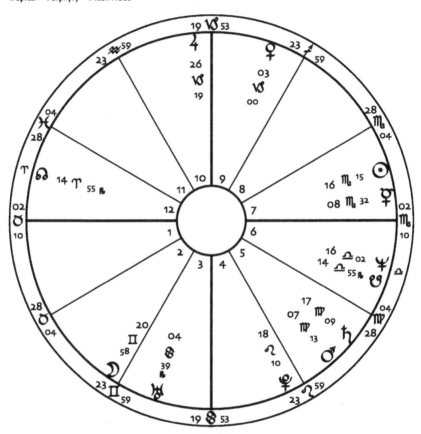

conjunct the Sun, sextile Pluto, trine Mars, sesquare Moon, opposite Uranus, and quincunx Jupiter.

Renowned opera singer Maria Callas had Venus square the nodes, opposite Pluto and widely square the Moon. Born in New York City, raised by an overbearing mother (Pluto square Moon), she received her musical education in Greece and established her career in Italy. Forced to deal with wartime poverty and myopia that left her nearly blind onstage, she endured struggles and scandal. Hailed as La Divina, Callas

John Coltrane
Natal Chart
September 23, 1926
5:00:00 PM EST
Hamlet, North Carolina
34N53 / 79W42
Tropical   Porphyry   Mean Node

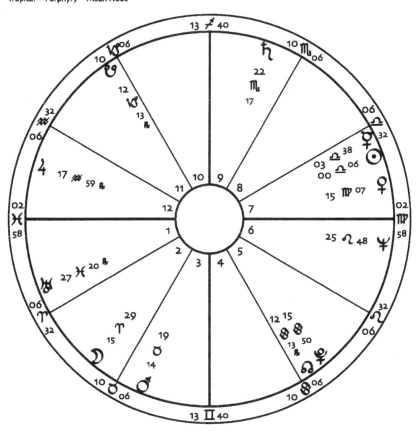

was known for her temperamental behavior, her rivalries, and her love affair with Greek tycoon Aristotle Onassis. Her Sun square Uranus and quincunx to Pluto in the 5th house signified her uniqueness, controversies, and powerful, momentous performances. Her artistic achievements were such that in 2006, Opera News wrote: "Nearly thirty years after her death, she's still the definition of the diva as artist—and still one of classical music's best-selling vocalists."

Classical guitar legend Andres Segovia was born at a New Moon

Maria Callas
Natal Chart
December 3, 1923
12:00:00 PM EST
New York, New York
40N43 / 74W00
Tropical   Porphyry   Mean Node

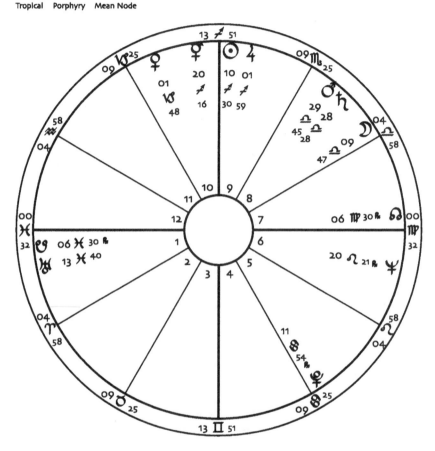

in Pisces conjunct Venus. Flamenco genius and innovator Paco de Lucia was born with Venus at the Ascendant in a Yod with Uranus and Saturn. The brilliant guitarist and composer Ralph Towner has Venus conjunct Jupiter, Saturn, and the south lunar node (Noon chart). Jazz guitarist Joe Pass had Sun semi-square Venus and Venus opposite Neptune (Noon chart). Wes Montgomery was born with Sun semi-square Venus and Venus square Mars (Noon chart).

Other planets besides Venus play a crucial role in music. For exam-

Andres Segovia

Natal Chart
March 17, 1893
6:30:00 PM LMT
Linares, Spain
38N05 / 3W38
Tropical   Porphyry   Mean Node

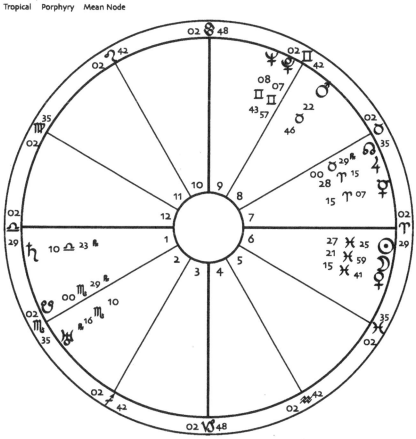

ple, Mercury signifies manual dexterity, playing with speed and facility, quickly and efficiently; it clarifies the articulation of notes, as well as lyrics that accompany music. Mars signifies the energy and drive within music, playing with energy force, volume, passion, fire. Mars also represents the demanding physicality required for singing or playing an instrument. Jupiter signifies a big sound, symphonic composition, an encompassing sound, large orchestration. Moon represents the *timbre*, the feeling and resonance of the sound or tone. Musicians learn to

Paco de Lucia
Natal Chart
December 21, 1947
9:54:00 AM CET
Alginet, Spain
39N16 / 0W28
Tropical   Porphyry   Mean Node

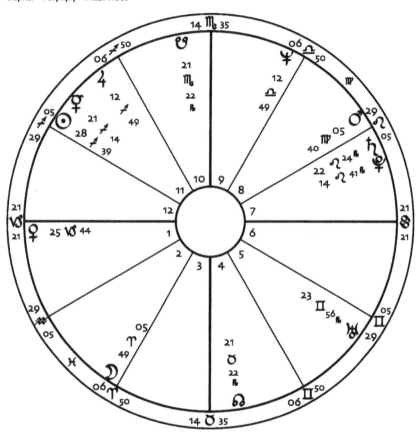

sound a note with a resonance that is clear and strong. Moon signifies living and playing music with feeling, like you really mean it. We have to put our whole body into whatever is happening in our charts so it resonates within us.

The great blues singer Bessie Smith had Moon opposite Venus and square Jupiter. Her professional mentor was the great Ma Rainey. They're two of the first publicly known black lesbian artists and they sang about women's experience (Moon-Venus-Jupiter). Neptune

Ralph Towner

Natal Chart
March 1, 1940
12:00:00 PM PST
Chehalis, Washington
46N40 / 122W58
Tropical   Porphyry   Mean Node

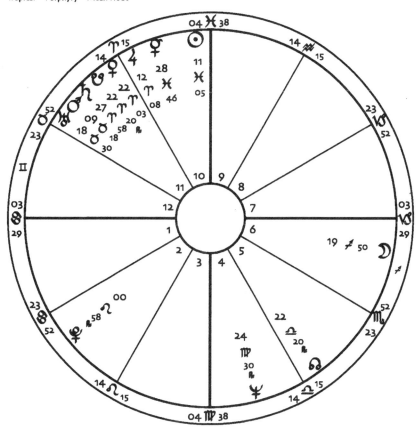

relates to music that has a melancholy air, a hint of sorrow, suffering, or lamentation. Bessie Smith's Sun in Aries opposed Saturn and was semi-square Neptune and Pluto in Gemini. Neptune corresponds to the sacred, salvational power of music, especially evident in the music of John Coltrane, who had Neptune square Mars and Saturn and opposite Jupiter in Aquarius in the 12th house, apt symbolism for a spiritual man whose magnetic energy and intensity advanced progressive music and expanded its social relevance.[72]

Joe Pass
Natal Chart
January 13, 1929
12:00:00 PM EST
New Brunswick, New Jersey
40N29 / 74W27
Tropical   Porphyry   Mean Node

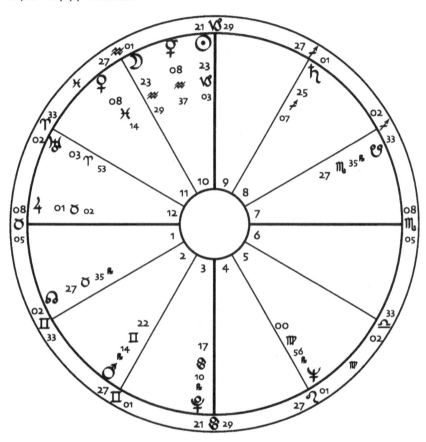

Under a strong Neptune influence we could be drawn to toning, space music, chanting, *bhajan*, Gregorian chant, ambient music. Neptune signifies ecstasy in music, the way one is carried away and lifted up in the act of musical performance. Tone, rhythm, song have been used for millennia to induce trance, ecstasies, and spiritual ascension. The astrological influence of Neptune corresponds to the space in music, music's capacity to uplift, to connect us to etheric planes—sound as a doorway to the imaginal, the spiritual realms. Sufi teacher Hazrat Inayat Khan said that music is:

Wes Montgomery

Natal Chart
March 6, 1923
12:00:00 PM CST
Indianapolis, Indiana
39N46 / 86W09
Tropical   Porphyry   Mean Node

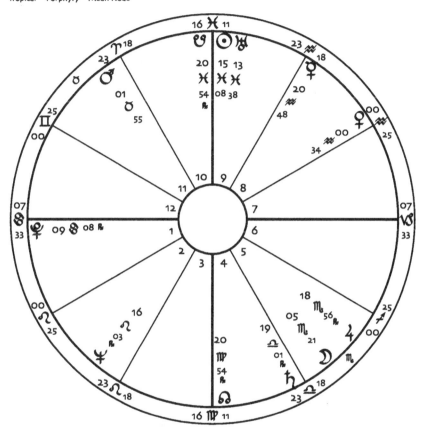

the bridge over the gulf between form and the formless. . . .
[Ancient people held the belief] that the creative source in
its first step toward manifestation was audible, and in its next
step visible. . . . [A]ll we see in this objective world, every form,
has been constructed by sound and is the phenomenon of
sound. . . . [T]he human body is a living resonator for sound.
. . . [T]he wise considered the science of sound to be the most
important science in every condition of life. In healing, in
teaching, in evolving, and in accomplishing all things in life.

Bessie Smith
Natal Chart
April 15, 1894
12:00:00 PM CST
Chattanooga, Tennessee
35N03 / 85W19
Tropical   Porphyry   Mean Node

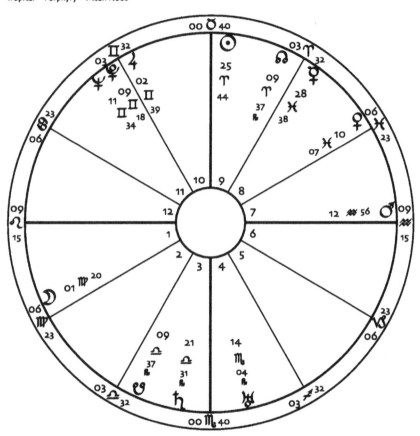

. . . [B]y the power of sound or word one can evolve spiritually and experience all the different stages of spiritual perfec-
tion. Music is the best medium for awakening the soul; there
is nothing better. Music is the shortest, the most direct way to
God. . . . Life is the outcome of harmony. At the back of the
whole creation is harmony, and the whole creation is harmony.
What man calls happiness, comfort, profit or gain, all he longs
for and wishes to attain is harmony. . . . And what does music

Hazrat Inayat Khan
Natal Chart
July 5, 1882
11:35:00 PM INOT
Baroda, India
22N18 / 73E12
Tropical   Porphyry   Mean Node

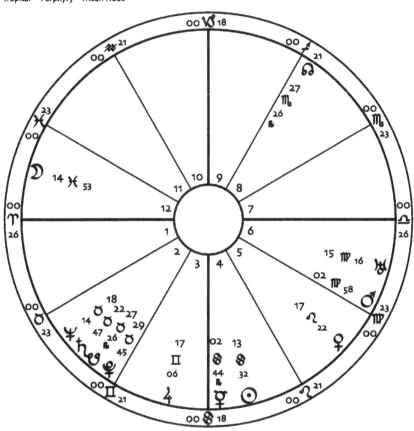

teach us? Music helps us train ourselves in harmony. . . . When you hear music that you enjoy, it tunes you and puts you in harmony with life. Therefore man needs music.[73]

I believe that astrology similarly trains us in harmony and tunes us to harmony.

Hazrat Inayat Khan had a close natal square of Venus and Neptune. He began his career as a performing musician (Venus in Leo in the 5th house), and experienced spiritual awakening through music. He entered ecstatic states while singing and playing the *veena* and felt that music and religious feeling were inseparable (natal Venus square Neptune).

Consonance and Dissonance

Studying natal aspects brings awareness of the personality as a totality, how different tones blend together as a chord, whether concordant or discordant. In western music we arrange individual tones into chords, which are built on major, minor, diminished, or augmented triads built on the first, third, and fifth notes of the scale. From there we add extensions, the 7th, 9th, 11th, and 13th notes from the tonic. Some chords are harmonious and consonant and some are dissonant and discordant. This is analogous to how in astrology inter-planetary aspects represent harmonious or dissonant chords.

Look at Inayat Khan's Sun trine Moon. An aspect such as this, or Sun trine Jupiter, might represent a harmonious, consonant chord, harmony and concordance within oneself, and an expansive sense of one's identity. Contrast that with Sun in hard aspect to Mars or Pluto or Uranus or Neptune, which might form a chord that's discordant or stressful, or represents challenges we face in achieving healthy self-esteem and self-expression. I know about this, having natal Sun in hard aspect to Uranus, Neptune, and Pluto. I recently spoke to a woman who had Taurus Sun in the 8th house opposing Uranus in her 2nd house. Her ex-husband was very down-to-earth financially, always concerned about saving money, while she earned a lot of money and liked to spend it freely. He was frustrated by the fact that she was rebellious, free-spirited (Sun-Uranus), not a compliant wife, which was what he'd expected. So that marriage could not hold.

Paradoxically, the harmony of life encompasses dissonance. Typically, we humans prefer ease and concordance but this can become static, inert, and boring—a dwelling in the status quo, the familiar, whereas dissonance in music and in life creates tension, urgency, and impetus for movement and change. Astrology recognizes the reality of conflict, tension, upheaval. We embrace the fact that there are stressful planetary contacts representing discordant tones, dissonant chords, and jarring life experiences. In my chart synastry with my wife Diana, my Mars squares her Moon and no matter how well we harmonize on many levels, there will always be moments of stress, conflict, disagreement, and emotional upset. These moments can't be avoided.

I relate the polarities of consonance versus dissonance, and also form versus improvisation to the interplay of Saturn and Uranus. Saturn has great significance for music as it represents the process of keeping time, staying on the beat, maintaining a steady rhythm. Saturn signifies poise, confidence, consistency, mastery of an instrument through self-discipline. It's a symbol of the conventional forms of music, playing within the structure of classical and folk music traditions.

Uranus represents vibrational shift, disturbance, or modulation—change to a new tonal key center. With Uranus, music speeds up, breaks established forms, and goes in a different direction. Thus, it's associated with progressive trends in music, the avant garde, jazz, electronica. Charlie Parker, the avatar of bebop, was born on a Full Moon in Pisces with a tight conjunction of Moon-Uranus opposing the Sun, Saturn, and Venus in Virgo. With Virgo Sun-Venus conjunct Saturn, Parker worked on his music with tireless self-discipline. With Sun opposite Uranus, he was an unstoppable force of melodic innovation and an unpredictable man whose raging Piscean heroin addiction led to numerous episodes of bizarre, disordered, unhinged behavior. But his music changed everything. He was a consummate artistic personality who exemplifies the Uranian individuation archetype.

John Coltrane had Uranus in his 1st house, opposite natal Sun, trine Saturn, and quincunx Neptune. Similarly, saxophonist Ornette Coleman had Sun conjunct Venus in Pisces, Mars semisquare Uranus, and Uranus square Saturn, signifying shattering the paradigm of jazz, reshaping jazz traditions. He evolved a new conception of jazz that was wholly original. French composer Claude Debussy also had Uranus square Saturn, as well as Moon applying to conjunction to Venus, and Venus trine Neptune. His music expressed a shimmering dissonance.

Ludwig van Beethoven had Uranus square Saturn, Venus conjunct

Charlie Parker
Natal Chart
August 29, 1920
1:45:00 AM CST
Kansas City, Kansas
39N07 / 94W38
Tropical   Porphyry   Mean Node

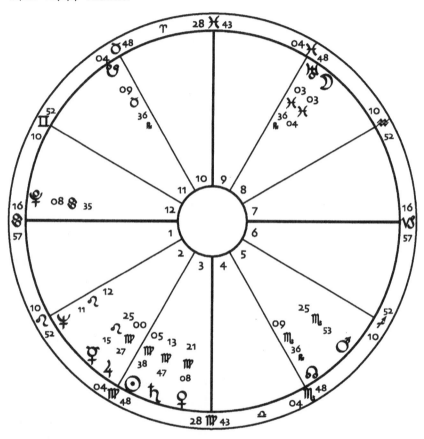

Pluto, and Mars in the 4th house opposite his Sun and Moon. He grew up in an atmosphere of extreme parental tension, family anxiety, and stress. His father taught him music in a brutal, intense, tyrannical fashion. Noel Tyl comments:

> Saturn is squared by Uranus in Taurus: any relationship between those planets is always a suggestion of there being new ways of doing things or the breaking away from tradition

Ornette Coleman
Natal Chart
March 9, 1930
5:00:00 AM CST
Fort Worth, Texas
32N44 / 97W19
Tropical   Porphyry   Mean Node

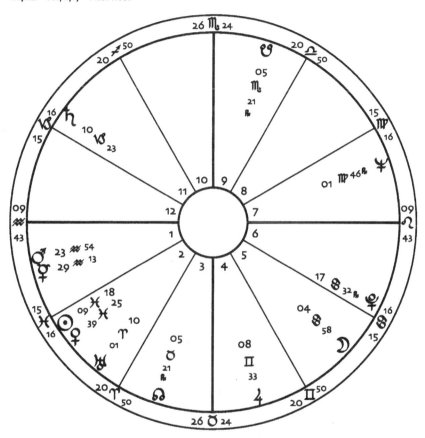

and embracing the avant garde; the modern, the new, and the different all beckon. . . . Uranus squares Saturn. . . . Uranus: the planet of electrifying individuality, rebellion, and genius. Beethoven was indeed a law for himself only to follow. . . . We see Beethoven as a powerhouse of Uranian impulse, eccentricity, and innovation. We seeing him fighting his way out of a household of rigor and misery, leaving it all behind, championing new ideas, and knowingly creating a new world of music." [74]

Claude Debussy

Natal Chart
August 22, 1862
4:30:00 AM LMT
St Germain, France
48N54 / 2E05
Tropical   Porphyry   Mean Node

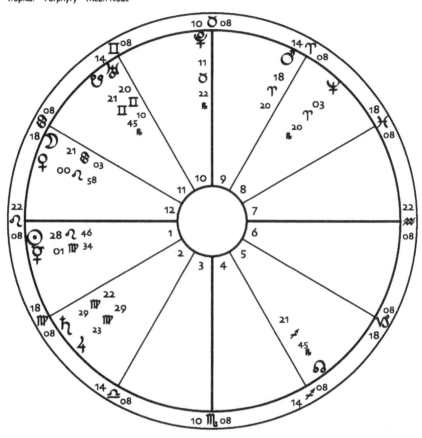

Uranus signifies the unconventional turn, revolutions, breakthroughs, rebellions in music, free jazz, atonalism in classical music. Bob Dylan has natal Uranus conjunct Saturn and Jupiter and widely conjunct his Sun. He's a unique, individuated artist who transformed American folk and rock music. Think of how Dylan was booed and criticized mercilessly when he went electric, shattering folk music conventions, in 1965 during the Uranus-Pluto conjunction, opposite Saturn in Pisces. This

Ludwig van Beethoven

Natal Chart
December 16, 1770
11:03:00 AM LMT
Bonn, Germany
50N44 / 7E05
Tropical   Porphyry   Mean Node

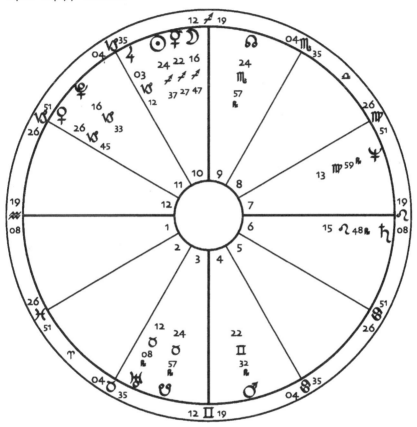

is how cultural innovation often begins—widely dismissed and vehemently resisted!

Significance of Uranus in the Astrology of Music and Culture

Uranus is especially important in understanding the astrology of music and culture. Richard Tarnas's book *Cosmos and Psyche* examines how outer planet alignments affect cultural trends and how archetypal complexes emerge in characteristic movements in the arts and culture. Tarnas identifies periods of heightened cultural creativity tied to phases of the cycles of Uranus-Pluto, which he associates with a "titanic quality[,] . . . Titanic impulse for change, titanic intensity and creativity, titanic struggle and defiance."[75] These qualities were evident during the Uranus-Pluto opposition of the 1790s, when Mozart, Haydn, Beethoven were at their peaks. This parallels trends during the Uranus-Pluto conjunction of the 1960s, the time of ascension of artists such as Dylan, the Beatles, Rolling Stones, Jimi Hendrix, and the Doors.

Also tied to periods of cultural creativity and artistic breakthroughs is the Jupiter-Uranus cycle. Tarnas notes that during the 1788 Jupiter-Uranus conjunction Mozart composed the Jupiter symphony and Haydn composed the Oxford Symphony, displaying new creative freedom. Tarnas calls this the summit of orchestral composition prior to Beethoven's Eroica (his 3rd Symphony). Composed during the Jupiter-Uranus conjunction of 1803 and soon after the Uranus-Pluto conjunction of the 1790s, Eroica was music expressing "the radical intensification of Promethean and Dionysian qualities . . . the heightened emancipatory drive, the titanic will to creative freedom, the intensity of turmoil and sudden unpredictable shifts, the unleashing of elemental forces, the awakening of nature's depths. . . ." [76]

The Uranus-Pluto Square: Sound of the Cosmos Evolving in Our Time

This turmoil and intensification of life, urge for emancipation from oppression, and unleashing of creative forces can be felt in our own era, as we're currently living through a period of changes occurring within the collective linked to the recent Uranus-Pluto square—which was exact from 2011 to 2016 and will continue to resonate in our world for years to come. According to Reinhold Ebertin, the planetary pair Uranus-Pluto signifies transformation and revolution, creative energy, innovations and reforms; upsets, destruction, and bringing new ideas and inventions into existence. It signifies pioneers, reformers, lives that are out of the ordinary.[77] Certainly many events are happening right now that are out of the ordinary. Immense upheavals and reforms are occurring in every sphere of life—in science, government, and econom-

Bob Dylan

Natal Chart
May 24, 1941
9:05:00 AM CST
Duluth, Minnesota
46N47 / 92W06
Tropical   Porphyry   Mean Node

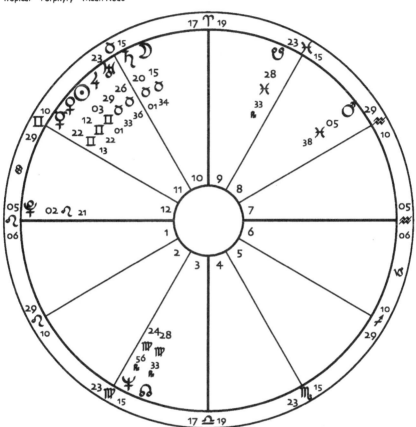

ics, in international relations, in church institutions and universities, in the fields of medicine and insurance, in human sexuality and patterns of bonding, and in the institutions of democracy. And a big question is whether we humans will be able to reorganize our whole way of living quickly enough to avoid environmental catastrophe and disruption of the order of nature.

The great British astrologer Charles Harvey noted that Uranus-Pluto signifies structural, institutional changes, "radical restructuring of peoples and nations."[78] The manifestations of this have been recently evident in Syria's brutal civil war and Assad's use of chemical weapons against his own people, ongoing war in Iraq, Yemen, and Somalia; Russia's annexation of Crimea and meddling in Ukraine; disputes over Israeli settlements and the nuclear deal with Iran; China building military bases on disputed islands and becoming increasingly assertive; North Korea testing missiles and threatening attacks; Fukushima and endless waves of radioactivity; weakening of the U. S. voting rights act; Russia's interference in the 2016 election and manipulation of American social media to aid the election of Donald Trump; and accelerating environmental degradation, climate change and species extinctions. The current energy on planet earth is quite intense. But astrologers are like surfers. We're not afraid of the big waves and high winds. We actually like them. In addition to the astrological analysis of our individual psychology and emotional dynamics, optimal vocational pathways, and archetypal themes shaping our development, we track outer planet transit cycles to understand our current social setting and historical circumstances, the story and the music of our time.

In *Cosmos and Psyche*, Tarnas studied the diachronic patterns of the Uranus-Pluto cycle, for example, the 1845–56 conjunction, 1896–1907 opposition, and the conjunction in 1963; and found that each phase corresponded to stages of women's movements, civil rights movements, struggles for freedom and equality, acts of civil disobedience, socialist movements, rise of countercultures and movements for social change, times of intellectual, scientific, and technological revolutions, periods of "social upheaval, political radicalism, and countercultural vitality."[79] Tarnas notes that Uranus liberates the Plutonic-Dionysian impulse, emancipating the erotic, libidinal dimensions of life, in sexual revolutions and loosening of restraints.[80] But under Uranus-Pluto aspects we also see "eruptions of the volcanic, violent, destructive elemental energies associated with the Dionysian-Plutonic-Kali principle."[81] Also, "a collective wave of disinhibition, a return of the repressed, that unleashed primitive, destructive forces."[82] We see this in incidents of human right abuses, senseless shootings and bombings in schools, places of worship, and shopping malls, the cruel violence of ISIS, people driving trucks into crowds, or assaulting strangers with knives and machetes, the return of swastikas and hate crimes, the emboldening of dictatorial forces, paranoia about immigrants, as well as the surfacing of massive amounts of plastic in oceans and sea creatures.

These are the background tones of our lives, a symphony of planetary upheaval. Knowing astrologers inwardly merge with the force of transformation symbolized by the square of Uranus and Pluto and find ways of channeling it. Uranus-Pluto suggests going beyond social convention and liberating ourselves to act in ways that are edgy, bold, and inventive. I've been writing books openly stating that psychotherapy and mental health care should employ astrology, yoga, meditation, dreams, and visualization, and asserting that these methodologies could be more powerful and efficacious for many people than psychiatric drugs—and definitely more integrative. In a profession dominated by the medical model, that isn't always a popular position to take, but I stand by it. This is my humble revolution.

In contemplating the natal chart and transits, one of our ultimate goals isn't just to actualize our individual pattern or archetype, to realize the Sun, but also to sound our own tone in resonance with the whole, with what's sounding in the collective sphere during this momentous planetary alignment. Uranus-Pluto can manifest as explosive discharges, agitated conditions, an unsettled atmosphere, intensified storm activity, strong forces of nature, high winds, destructive fires, earthquakes and volcanic eruptions. This climate of stormy, moody intensity is also reflected in emotional ordeals people are going through, as evidenced by the growing prevalence of depression, anxiety, bipolar disorder, and addictions. But if we're able to maintain the stabilizing structures of Saturn and to self-regulate our emotions to avoid drastic mood swings, and closely follow our celestial instructions, the wise amongst us will respond to the evolutionary challenge of our times, becoming conduits for the energy of innovation, discovery, and systems evolution, inwardly merging with the creative power, the *maha shakti* of Pluto-Uranus. We need to find healthy modes of energy charge and discharge (for me, it's through exercise and music), and to allow ourselves to be infused with the universe's dynamism, so we can become vehicles for the archetypes of transformation to manifest.

Uranus square Pluto represents *pranic* and motivational activation, shaktic awakening, and raising our energy. It's good to get your life force moving through muscular exertion of any kind. Breathe, pump some weights, stretch, spin, swim, run, build core strength. Oxygenate. That's how you can get into a clear mind space and use this alignment to strengthen your vital power. What I personally find most useful in this regard is to practice the yogic breath of fire, *bhastrika pranayama*, which charges the *prana*.[83] Intonate your body and do what resonates. Focus the energy that's coming in and coming through. Visualize and feel for a moment that a great power and vitality is within you, urging you to act with focus and determination. With this alignment involving Uranus and Pluto, everything is changing into a different form. It's a time filled with a powerful *mana* or vital energy. In various languages 'mana' means 'thunder, storm, or wind,' powerful forces of nature. Under the Uranus-Pluto square the atmosphere in our world has become in many ways quite unpleasant, disturbing, and dissonant, as well as more divisive and mistrustful. Our discussion of career challenges and crises touched on this. The key to enlightened response is to be aligned with our own birth pattern and thus to create our own force field of action. For conscious astrologers who catch the wave, who feel the thunder and storm winds of spirit, the Uranus-Pluto square can represent expanding our magnetic influence, becoming a force for creative evolution.

My client Penelope has natal Sun in Aries in the 6th house, in a Yod involving Neptune at the Ascendant and Uranus-Pluto in Virgo in her 11th house. Aligned with that powerful natal conjunction in the house of political awareness and group activity, she works for social justice, addressing human rights abuses and human trafficking through diplomacy and advocacy and counseling of the victims. With Sun trine Jupiter in Leo in the 10th house, she's a teacher who spreads joy. Aptly expressing her 6th house Sun, she teaches job-seeking skills to homeless immigrants. She feels called to this work, even though it requires long hours, modest compensation, and much dedication. Her Sun is in Yod alignment with all three outer planets. A Yod indicates a tension that requires adjustments. At the time of our consultation, transiting Uranus was conjunct her Sun for several months as it turned stationary direct in the final degrees of Aries. Penelope is at a point of conflict in her workplace as she wants to innovate, individuate, and do things her

Penelope

Natal Chart
April 15, 1968
Tropical   Porphyry   Mean Node

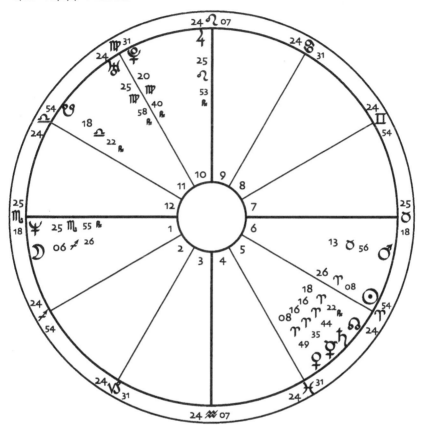

own way (Uranus-Sun), but she has to operate within the constraints of large institutions and bureaucracies (Pluto in 11th house). She wants to leave her job to have more freedom (Uranus conjunct natal Sun) but she also wants to be a part of this work and enterprise, and this job is a place where she can realize that objective of working for social change. She has had to swallow her pride and neutralize her Sun's tendency to feel insulted and huffy (Sun trine Jupiter in Leo) about being asked to conform to certain workplace policies and protocols (Uranus-Pluto in Virgo: the experience of workers and impersonal corporate guidelines). Penelope chooses to stay in the struggle, and even though it's uncomfortable there's no place she'd rather be. She can't afford to be too headstrong (Aries Sun) and risk losing this opportunity to do something of social significance. She's very much involved and invested in this work, while Uranus is conjunct her 6th house Sun. She is training others, passing on skills (6th house), and also expressing her caring nature and the altruistic social vocational interests symbolized by Moon and Neptune conjunct her Ascendant.

Uranus and Pluto also represent clearing, getting rid of what you don't really need, clearing space, and undergoing radical change and transformation. Here's an example of radical and sudden change. After years of placating and enabling her alcoholic husband, a woman named Terri carried out an intervention. She hired a professional interventionist to come into her home and assembled in the living room every friend, colleague, and family member close to her husband, to tell him how much they love him; how they've been affected by his drinking; and what will be the consequences if he doesn't stop immediately. He completed a 5-day detox in a hospital and a 28-day inpatient rehab program, then spent two months in a halfway house. He came home a changed man, ready to begin a new phase. I admire Terri and her family for their courage to take these radical steps for change. They went out on a limb, seeking nothing less than a state of redemption. Sometimes a radical change is needed. Noel Tyl interprets Uranus-Pluto as over-turning the status quo.[84] This intervention is an example of successfully mobilizing the will to change. Terri utilized a firm and loving form of coercion, and it worked. That's a good example of the positive expression of Pluto, applying force of will for conscious change.

I experienced this empowerment recently in a different sphere of life as transiting Pluto has made a two-year pass over the Nadir of my chart—my Capricorn 4th house cusp. I'll admit that initially I was slightly fearful of the possible destructive mayhem that could result from Pluto transiting the IC. What actually happened is that after 26 years living in the same neighborhood of the same city, my wife and I made the decision that we wanted a larger house, a safer neighborhood, and also to distance ourselves from a neighbor with whom it was difficult to maintain harmonious relations. We simply needed to move. For a year we renovated our existing house, doing some demolition and remodeling. There was much loud drilling and removal of concrete slabs and other construction debris. We thereby increased the value of the house so that it sold it for a much higher price than we anticipated. This gave us a good amount of cash toward the purchase of a larger, more elegant home, built in 1932, with Mediterranean features, including beams, arches, and columns that make the house feel like a Spanish villa. This move occurred at the third pass of Pluto (ruler of my 2nd house: finances and purchases) in Capricorn (older structures and traditional or classical design features) conjunct the IC.

Making all of this happen required the astute business acumen of our realtor (Pluto: knowing how to work a deal and play it skillfully) and the constant effort my wife and I made to sustain our respective business and professional activities (transiting Saturn and Pluto in Capricorn) to assure the continuing flow of money to pay for the house and extensive renovations. During our first six months of residency (during the fourth pass of Pluto over the Nadir) we addressed issues with gutters, plumbing, termite damage to decks, burrowing rodents in the yard (voles), expanded a stone patio, rebuilt two staircases, and completed a seismic upgrade that involved digging seven pits under the house down to the bedrock and pouring concrete piers to shore up the foundation, strengthening the support beams under the house, and bolting the house more securely. All of this reflected Pluto's transit over the Nadir, the point of foundations. Then we excavated the entire yard to create a new irrigation and drainage system, and finally planted the beginning of a new garden, just in time for the autumn rains. It took two years of hard work to engineer a change of residence and during all of it I was aware of Pluto demolishing and reconstructing my domestic life structures. I continued working with this process during the fifth and final pass of Pluto conjunct IC, which lasted about six months, at which time we completed renovation of our ground floor to transform the space into a home office, where I'm now conducting some of my counseling practice. Despite my initial trepidation, during this three-year transit to my Nadir I hit the jackpot on a nice house in a good location. It has been one more lesson in practical magic.

At every moment, astrology helps us gain understanding of what's happening to us. As this book goes to press our world is greatly changed by the Coronavirus. The year 2020 features immensely powerful, stressful transits, notably the conjunction of Mars-Jupiter-Saturn-Pluto in Capricorn. Mars conjunct Pluto and Saturn is the symbol of the pandemic and marks its inception. Pluto signifies viruses and infectious disease. Mars can be an inflammatory influence. The Mars-Pluto conjunction marks the spread of this nasty infection. The Saturn-Pluto conjunction represents imposition of strict controls, our need to endure difficult circumstances, to simplify and strip down to the basics. As I write this, Saturn has just entered Aquarius so we're suddenly faced with developing a new consciousness that demands we think and act as a collective, as cooperative groups. Right now we have to bear down and accomplish whatever we can at home. I have faith that good can come out of this if we're able to stay healthy and respond with calm, poise, equanimity, and exercise both our interdependence and our capacity for self-sufficiency. Jupiter will be conjunct Pluto in Capricorn throughout 2020. This denotes the emergence of strong personalities capable of taking on big tasks of management, organization, and positive leadership. Now, during this world crisis, our study and practice of astrology is a trustworthy guide to steer ourselves through every storm.

Wise astrologers choose how to sound a tone in the universe—to be an emanating source, a creator. The current 2020 Jupiter-Saturn-Pluto conjunction in Capricorn and early Aquarius is an opportunity to take significant steps toward accomplishment in our personal enterprises and participation in progressive social evolution.

Astrology gives us the tools to make our life a measured composition with many voices unfolding in harmonious counterpoint—to live consciously in multiple domains, and to tap the higher octaves of our human capacities. It strengthens our sense of agency and conscious participation in every facet and moment of personal evolution—so our life becomes an unending wave of evolutionary spirals.

Endnotes

1 G. Bogart, *Dreamwork and Self-Healing* (London: Routledge, 2009); and *Dreamwork in Holistic Psychotherapy of Depression* (London: Routledge, 2017).

2 This topic is explored in G. Bogart, *Astrology and Spiritual Awakening* (2nd edition) (Tempe, AZ: AFA Books, 2014).

3 For delineation of the Jupiter-Saturn conjunction through the 12 houses see *Astrology and Meditation: The Fearless Contemplation of Change* (Bournemouth, U. K.: Wessex Astrologer), pp. 125–34.

4 I read everything I could get my hands on by C. G. Jung, M. L. von Franz, and James Hillman.

5 I. Goldstein-Jacobsen, *Simplified Horary Astrology* (Anchorage, AK: Frank Severy Publishing, 1975).

6 At the present time, I'm keenly anticipating the upcoming Jupiter-Saturn conjunction in December 2020 at 0° Aquarius 31, and recommend that every astrologer examine where this planetary alignment activates the natal chart.

7 G. Bogart, *Therapeutic Astrology: Using the Birth Chart in Psychotherapy and Spiritual Counseling* (Berkeley, CA: Dawn Mountain Press, 1996).

8 G. Bogart, *Planets in Therapy: Predictive Technique and the Art of Counseling* (Lake Worth, FL: Ibis, 2012).

9 See the discussion of conscious suffering in *Astrology and Meditation*, op cit., pp. 98–103.

10 G. Bogart, *Planets in Therapy*, op cit.

11 These mandala diagrams first appeared in *Astrology and Spiritual Awakening*, op cit., where I discussed the "Twelve Yogas of the Zodiac" in detail. The wording has been updated for this current discussion.

12   For more on this point, see G. Bogart, *Astrology and Meditation*, op cit.

13   See *Planets in Therapy*, op cit., pp. 59–62.

14   D. Polkinghorne, *Narrative Knowing and the Human Sciences* (Albany, NY: State University of New York Press, 1988), pp. 126, 145, 150, 152.

15   L. Cochran, *Life-Shaping Decisions* (New York: Lang, 1991); L. Cochran, *Career Counseling: A Narrative Approach* (Newbury Park, CA: Sage Publications, 1997).

16   L. Cochran, *Career Counseling: A Narrative Approach,* op cit.

17   For a full explanation of this point, see "Rudhyar's Astrology in Plain Language," in *Planets in Therapy*, op cit.

18   See *Planets in Therapy*, op cit., pp. 314–19.

19   For a comprehensive vision of the astrology of history and the evolution of culture, see R. Tarnas, *Cosmos and Psyche* (New York: Viking, 2006).

20   I described a poignant personal example of this in *Planets in Therapy*, op cit., pp. 252–58.

21   C. G. Jung, Archetypes of the Collective Unconscious. *Collected Works, Volume 9* (Princeton, NJ: Bollingen, 1934/1959), par. 322.

22   Ibid, par. 304.

23   E. Whitmont & S. Perera, *Dreams: A Portal to the Source* (Toronto: Inner City, 1989), pp. 17–8.

24   M. Hyde, *Jung and Astrology* (London: Aquarian Press, 1992).

25   See "Synastry and Conscious Relationships" in *Planets in Therapy*, op cit., pp. 261–81.

26   C. G. Jung, Letter to Andres Barbault. *Letters* (London: Routledge Kegan Paul, 1954), p. 177.

27   R. Aziz, *C. G. Jung's Psychology of Religion and Synchronicity* (Albany, NY: State University of New York Press, 1990), p. 53.

28   A. Stevens, *Archetype Revisited: An Updated Natural History of the Self* (Toronto, Inner City, 2003), p. 14.

29 Cited by A. Stevens, *Archetype Revisited*, op cit., p. 14.

30 A. Stevens, *Archetype Revisited*, op cit., p.16.

31 Ibid, pp. 17–8.

32 Ibid, pp. 43–4, 46.

33 D. Rudhyar, *Astrology and the Modern Psyche* (Sebastopol, CA, CRCS, 1976), p. 31. I'm indebted to my friend Nick Campion for first pointing out to me the significance of this passage.

34 G. Hill, *Masculine and Feminine* (Boston: Shambhala, 1992), pp. 25–6.

35 G. Bogart, *Dreamwork in Holistic Psychotherapy of Depression*, op cit., and *Dreamwork and Self-Healing*, op cit.

36 D. Rudhyar, *The Sun is Also a Star* (Santa Fe, NM, Aurora Press, 1982).

37 M. Stein, *Jung's Map of the Soul* (La Salle, IL: Open Court), p. 142.

38 M. L. von Franz, *On Divination and Synchronicity: The Psychology of Meaningful Chance* (Toronto: Inner City, 1980), pp. 7–9, 14, 71.

39 Ibid, p. 62.

40 The term "felt sense" comes from the work of Eugene Gendlin, originator of the Focusing method. See E. Gendlin, *Focusing-Oriented Psychotherapy: A Manual of the Experiential Method* (New York, Guildford, 1998).

41 C. Lunz, *Vocational Guidance by Astrology* (St. Paul, MN: Llewellyn, 1942).

42 N. Tyl (Ed.). *Vocational Astrology for Success in the Workplace* (St. Paul, MN: Llewellyn, 1992).

43 C. Lunz, *Vocational Guidance by Astrology*, op cit., p. 231.

44 N. Tyl, *Vocations: The New Midheaven Extension Process* (Minneapolis: Llewellyn, 2006).

45 F. Cossar-Blake, *Vocational Astrology: Finding the Right Career*

Direction (London: LSA/Flare, 2017); J. Hill, *Vocational Astrology* (Tempe, AZ: American Federation of Astrologers, 1997).

46   In the spring of 1980, I was sitting in on a couple of Allen Ginsberg's poetry classes at Naropa Institute. One day he saw me with a guitar and asked me if I could accompany him at a concert. He said, "Come to my house tomorrow." The next day I rehearsed a few songs with him over at his house and it sounded horrible. The music and his voice just didn't connect. But Allen said, "Don't worry, we'll rehearse again on stage." Once we were on stage in front of everybody the performance went off smoothly, without a hitch. We performed two songs flawlessly. On another occasion Allen came walking down Pearl Street where I was sitting strumming my guitar. He asked me, "Why aren't ya' workin'?" I'll always remember the irony of having the world's most famous bohemian poet telling me to 'get a job'! Then he asked me if I could play a blues in the key of C. I hit it, and he launched into an absolutely shocking song called Dope Fiend Blues, then segued into a loud rant about the CIA and the JFK assassination, as a crowd gathered in the streets gaping at him. Here was the embodiment of the bard, in the flesh. Befitting his Mars-Uranus conjunction on the Ascendant, Allen was hilarious, outrageous, and completely uninhibited. A few weeks later Allen spent a half hour reading a poem I'd written about my 1978 voyage in India and making some suggestions. In a few minutes, he taught me an essential lesson about how to write. He said, "What do you mean here? Why do you use these abstract terms? Less philosophizing. Tell me what actually happened, what you really saw and felt. Pay more attention to concrete facts and details." He told me, "Stay close to the nose" and focus on what William Carlos Williams calls the "concrete particulars." The poem was later published in my book, *Finding Your Life's Calling* (Berkeley, CA: Dawn Mountain Press, 1995).

47   I addressed this topic in the sections on "Gifts of Saturn" in *Planets in Therapy,* op cit., and "Saturn and the Practical Business of Life" in *Astrology and Spiritual Awakening,* op cit.

48   Plotinus, cited in Joachim-Ernst Berendt, *Nada Brahma: The World is Sound: Music and the Landscape of Consciousness* (Rochester, VT: Destiny Books, 1983), p. 65.

49   Kepler, cited in Berendt, *Nada Brahma*, op cit., p. 65.

50   J. Godwin, *Music, Mysticism, and Magic: A Sourcebook* (New York and London: Arkana, 1986), p. 14.

51   Ibid, p. 119.

52   Berendt, *Nada Brahma*, op cit., p. 60.

53   Ibid, p. 63.

54   Ibid, pp. 64–5.

55   Ibid, pp. 58–9.

56   Title page from Basil Valentine: *Revelation des mysteres des teintures essentielles des sept metaux* (Paris, 1668).

57   A. Faivre, "Introduction." In A. Faivre & J. Needleman (Eds.), *Modern Esoteric Spirituality* (New York: Crossroads Publishing, 1995), pp. xii–xiii.

58   Ibid, p. v.

59   Ibid, p. xv.

60   Ibid, p. xvi.

61   Ibid, pp. xvii–xviii.

62   D. Rudhyar, *The Magic of Tone and the Art of Music*. Boston: Shambhala, 1982, p. 6.

63   Ibid, pp. 8–9, 11–13.

64   This is the cover photo from D. Rudhyar, *The Magic of Tone and the Art of Music*, op cit.

65   Ibid, p. 40.

66   D. Rudhyar, *The Practice of Astrology as a Technique of Human Understanding* (Baltimore, MD: Penguin, 1968), pp. 29, 37.

67   Ibid.

68   Berendt, *Nada Brahma*, op cit., pp. 15–18.

69   A. Ruperti, *Cycles of Becoming* (Sebastopol, CA: CRCS, 1978).

70   For discussion of the art of synastry, see *Planets in Therapy*, op cit.

71   See "Transpersonal Astrology and the Path of Transformation" in *Astrology and Spiritual Awakening*, op cit.

72   See G. Bogart, *Astrology and Spiritual Awakening*, op cit., pp. 134–35.

73   Hazrat Inayat Khan, cited in J. Godwin, *Music, Mysticism, and Magic*, op cit., pp. 261–63, 265.

74   N. Tyl, *The Astrology of the Famed* (Minneapolis: Llewellyn, 1996), pp. 308–09, 322.

75   R. Tarnas, *Cosmos and Psyche*, op cit., p. 198.

76   R. Tarnas, *Cosmos and Psyche*, op cit., p. 318. A similarly heightened period of musical creativity occurred when the 1960s reached a crescendo as Uranus came into conjunction with Jupiter in Libra, right after the Uranus-Pluto conjunction. This Jupiter-Uranus conjunction, exact between December 1968 through August 1969, coincided with release of unforgettable music by artists such as: Beatles (Hello Goodbye, Revolution, Hey Jude, Get Back), Steppenwolf (Born to Be Wild), Otis Redding (Sitting by the Docks of the Bay), Rolling Stones (Jumping Jack Flash), Simon and Garfunkel (Mrs. Robinson), Donovan (Hurdy Gurdy Man), Credence Clearwater Revival (Suzie Q), Mason Williams (Classical Gas), Rascals (People Got to be Free), Doors (Hello I Love You), Marvin Gaye (I Heard it Through the Grapevine), Led Zeppelin (Whole Lotta Love), Sly and the Family Stone (Everyday People), Who (Tommy), Neil Young (Cinnamon Girl, Down by the River), and Santana (Evil Ways). During this time frame the film Easy Rider was released, the Woodstock music festival happened, and Elvis topped the U.S. Charts with Suspicious Minds.

77   R. Ebertin, *The Combination of Stellar Influences* (Aalen Germany: Ebertin Verlag, 1972), p. 198.

78   C. Harvey, "Cycles in Practice," in M. Baigent, N. Campion, C. Harvey, *Mundane Astrology* (Wellingborough. U.K.: Aquarian Press, 1984), p. 181.

79 R. Tarnas, *Cosmos and Psyche*, op cit., p. 156.

80 Ibid, pp. 166–67.

81 Ibid, p. 168.

82 Ibid, p. 169.

83 I discuss this practice in my book *In the Company of Sages* (Rochester, VT: Inner Traditions, 2015), pp. 240–45.

84 N. Tyl, *Prediction in Astrology* (St. Paul, MN: Llewellyn, 1995), pp. 319, 299.

About the Author

Greg Bogart, PhD, MFT is a psychotherapist and astrologer in private practice in Berkeley and El Cerrito, California, and a lecturer in psychology at Sonoma State University. A native of New York City, Greg graduated from Wesleyan University and eventually relocated to the San Francisco Bay Area, where he studied at California Institute of Integral Studies (CIIS), Saybrook University, and the Iyengar Yoga Institute of San Francisco. He taught for 20 years in the counseling psychology graduate programs at CIIS, John F. Kennedy University, Dominican University, and the Institute of Transpersonal Psychology. Greg is a licensed Marriage and Family Therapist, an ISAR Certified Astrological Professional, and holds NCGR Level IV certification as an astrological counselor. His books include *Astrology and Spiritual Awakening, Planets in Therapy, In the Company of Sages, Dreamwork and Self-Healing, Dreamwork in Holistic Psychotherapy of Depression,* and *Astrology and Meditation: The Fearless Contemplation of Change.*

Websites: www.dawnmountain.com and www.gregbogart.net.